2 *Pause and P...*

A Biblically-based Devotional

Book III

Your Free Book is Waiting!

Are you seeking to develop a more intimate Prayer Life with Jesus? Do you want to know what God's Word says about Prayer? Then this beautifully illustrated book is for you!

This "Pray-it-Through" verse style of Devotional combines a Word Search Puzzle, Sketch Art, and full-size Coloring Pages to create an innovative way 2 Pause and Praise the Lord. This 72-page offering is a prequel for Deb's other full-size Word Search Puzzle Books. On Wings of Prayer will deepen your conversations with the Lord. Here, you'll be encouraged to get into God's Word and sink His precious truths into your heart!

Get your free copy of *On Wings of Prayer* here:

There's a Song in the Air Devotional
Copyright 2023 © 2 Pause and Praise Creations

Requests for information should be directed to:
Deborah Goshorn-Stenger
2 Pause and Praise Creations
5315 Long Street, Suite 518
McFarland, WI 53558

ISBN: 978-1-954690-24-0

"The shepherds told everyone what had happened and what the angel had said to them about this child. All who heard the shepherds' story expressed astonishment, but Mary quietly treasured these things in her heart and often thought about them. Then the shepherds went back again to their fields and flocks, praising God for the visit of the angels, and because they had seen the child, just as the angel had told them." Luke 2:17-20 TLB

Our mission is to share the love of Jesus through His Word, nature, and creativity. We believe that God's beauty is all around us, if we'll pause to see it, and give Him honor and praise.

Preface

It's Christmas time and *There's a Song in the Air.* Step into the celebration by experiencing Jesus' birth from the vantage point of various Biblical characters, the Gospel Accounts, favorite Carol Titles, and by traveling through the Word to unwrap the Good News of Jesus' mission and ministry.

This unique Devotional presents original "Pray-it-Through" style meditations to gently guide your quiet time with the Lord. Each section features 8 verses that expand upon the story and mission of Jesus' birth and life through a Carol Title. These related Scriptures will take you on a rich journey throughout the Bible. Each section also features a special Bible study pertaining to the carol's topic.

Dear Jesus, may Your Spirit open my mind in a fresh way to the story of Your birth in this holy season. As I come into Your presence to know more of You, may You fill my heart with a song of joy. Let each verse, prayer, and reading teach me the gift of stillness and bring me peace. And let me share these gifts generously, I pray. Amen.

From
Deborah's
Heart

We had dinner with our Life Group from our church in July (of this year). As we gathered around two circular tables, sharing our week, Doug and I were asked about our current "projects." I told them that I "am working on a Christmas Devotional." They were teasing me about it being "Christmas in July." We laughed and answered, "Yes."

Then, one of the guys asked, "How early do you decorate for Christmas?" I told him ... "Usually, around the first of November, we put up our inside decorations, and since it gets way below freezing in Wisconsin, we put our outside decorations up around mid-November. However, we don't light them until Thanksgiving week."

Then he asked how long we keep it up. In answer, honestly, this varies. I shared that I prefer a winter theme as opposed to red/green. I like changing the theme yearly, varying the tree and garland with snowflakes, stars, and icicles, and adding other ornaments. We've taken decorations down as early as 6 January or as late as Easter, depending on the year and our circumstances. And we always put on Christmas music, which makes this a tradition and feels like a way to bless our home.

From the time I was a child, I have always had a happy heart that likes to hum and sing. So, Christmas finds my heart especially joyful since it celebrates Jesus' birth and life. In fact, music has always played an impactful role in my life. My mom often joked that I was born singing. Whether at home, in church, or school programs, I've always loved to give the Lord praise and honor. So, *There's a Song in the Air* is a natural extension of my heart's desire and life theme.

5

This unique telling of Jesus' birth will be more than the unfolding of the manger scene. These "Pray-it-Through" Scripture meditations—from throughout the Bible—have been specifically chosen to invite you into the mission and ministry of Who Jesus is to discover the risen King through His Titles, His power, majesty, sovereignty, and will go on to demonstrate to your heart how these relate to your life.

The inspiration for *There's a Song in the Air* came from my quiet time with the Lord and the praise that plays a part in each day. As I began to think about all the beautiful Titles of Carols, I pondered verses that would highlight and bring out the Luke 2 account and these beloved favorites.

There's a Song in the Air,
It echoes on the breeze,
Bringing Good News and tidings,
Which weave through the branches and the leaves.
It lifts high into the atmosphere,
To waft into the starry sky;
The Christ-child has come tonight,
And all of heaven's drawing nigh.
The shepherds and the Wisemen,
The saints and angels all proclaim,
The Messiah is born,
Come honor and praise His holy name.
Let us exalt Him,
Let us celebrate,
The birthday of King Jesus,
Our beloved Potentate.
Let us bow in worship;
And gather 'round His throne,
On this blessed Christmas day,
And forever 'til we're home.

Dear heart, Jesus the Babe is beckoning you
to know Him as Messiah and as Your personal
Lord and dearest Friend, this Christmas season!
In His love, deborah

Table of Contents

Prequel

From Mary's Journal: A fictional account of her Thoughts at the time of Jesus' Birth:

The road has been dusty. We're both exhausted from the journey from Nazareth to Bethlehem. My belly's swollen, heavy with the coming babe, the One Who the angel proclaimed would be the very Son of God. Joseph has been so loving and caring of us. He's been so attentive to our needs. When we finally arrived in this little village, he went from place to place seeking lodging. I could feel my time drawing near; how I cried out to the Lord for help!

Joseph left me for a few minutes to rest as he continued to knock on the doors. He returned with the news that our bed for the night would not be at the candlelit inn but instead in the cattle stall that stood behind it. He shared that our beds would not be hay and down-filled mattresses but the hay itself. But at that point, any bed sounded good, so with gratitude and weariness, I took his arm to find our place. Night was closing in, and we were glad to be off our feet. So was our donkey; he, too, was ready to collapse.

We unloaded our small pack of belongings, had a bit to eat, and settled in for the night. It was so beautiful there despite the imperfect conditions. The cattle stall was set in such a way as to give us a perfect view of the moon and starry canopy. I could feel God's presence so vividly, as if these gave us an intimate space to commune with Him alone. Joseph put his arm around me to comfort myself and the babe, and we drifted off to sleep that way. It was a Silent Night indeed. Praise came easily to my heart.

How thankful I was to Jehovah for His lovingkindness toward us. How blessed we were to be chosen to be His vessels for this wondrous event. Holy is He Who is King of our hearts.

In the wee hours, I had begun to stir from the birth pains. Joseph was awakened by my tossing to and fro. I knew we would soon meet this Child Whom Gabriel told us to name Jesus. As the hours went on, my prayers grew in intensity in time with the cramping and spasms. Finally, with one last push, Joseph helped me deliver the Christ-child. His cry split the night, and we laughed and cried with joy. From the confines of this tiny space, we knew we were part of a miracle. And how I pondered all the events of the past months. I cherished them to take them out individually in later days and over the coming years.

One Silent Night, I was a servant to the Most High God by bringing His Son into the world via the Holy Spirit who rested upon me. It was too astounding for me to put into words. Yet, my heart was filled with awe and exclamations unto my Savior as Joseph and I dreamed of how this Child would change the world. As I drifted off to sleep with happiness and exhaustion once again, I worshiped. Think of it, Jesus, the One who came to save all people from their sins, was lying safely in the manger. I felt so many emotions; it's been difficult to articulate them in these few lines, but simply holding Him in my arms was glorious. I know I'll have much to learn and surrender to the Messiah, but on that night, I was at peace, and somehow, it will always be set apart in my mind as holy.

The Biblical Account of Jesus' Birth

"Now in those days a decree went out from Caesar Augustus, that a census be taken of all the inhabited earth. This was the first census taken while Quirinius was governor of Syria. And all the people were on their way to register for the census, each to his own city. Now Joseph also went up from Galilee, from the city of Nazareth, to Judea, to the city of David which is called Bethlehem, because he was of the house and family of David, in order to register along with Mary, who was betrothed to him, and was pregnant. While they were there, the time came for her to give birth. And she gave birth to her firstborn son; and she wrapped Him in cloths, and laid Him in a manger, because there was no room for them in the inn.

In the same region there were some shepherds staying out in the fields and keeping watch over their flock at night. And an angel of the Lord suddenly stood near them, and the glory of the Lord shone around them; and they were terribly frightened. And so the angel said to them, 'Do not be afraid; for behold, I bring you good news of great joy which will be for all the people; for today in the city of David there has been born for you a Savior, who is Christ the Lord. And this will be a sign for you: you will find a baby wrapped in cloths and lying in a manger.' And suddenly there appeared with the angel a multitude of the heavenly army of angels praising God and saying ...

'Glory to God in the highest, and on earth peace among people with whom He is pleased.'

When the angels had departed from them into heaven, the shepherds began saying to one another, 'Let's go straight to Bethlehem, then, and see this thing that has happened, which the Lord has made known to us.' And they came in a hurry and found their way to Mary and Joseph, and the baby as He lay in the manger. When they had seen Him, they made known the statement which had been told them about this Child. And all who heard it were amazed about the things which were told them by the shepherds. But Mary treasured all these things, pondering them in her heart. And the shepherds went back, glorifying and praising God for all that they had heard and seen, just as had been told them." Luke 2:1-20 (NASB)

We Have Angels Heard On High
○ ○ ○

A Meditation on
Angels We Have Heard On High

I love "looking into" the scenes that Scripture illustrates for us, especially the birth of Jesus. I have found this to be one of the sweetest ways in which the Spirit has taught me. When we read God's Word from the vantage point of its participants and characters—we gain understanding and wisdom into the Lord's heart.

Take the angelic visitations that surrounded His arrival, for instance. Matthew 1:18-25 sets the stage for how Joseph was informed that he would be a daddy.

"This is how Jesus the Messiah was born. His mother, Mary, was engaged to be married to Joseph. But before the marriage took place, while she was still a virgin, she became pregnant through the power of the Holy Spirit. Joseph, to whom she was engaged, was a righteous man and did not want to disgrace her publicly, so he decided to break the engagement quietly. As he considered this, an angel of the Lord appeared to him in a dream. 'Joseph, son of David,' the angel said, 'do not be afraid to take Mary as your wife. For the child within her was conceived by the Holy Spirit. And she will have a son, and you are to name him Jesus, for he will save his people from their sins.' All of this occurred to fulfill the Lord's message through his prophet: 'Look! The virgin will conceive a child! She will give birth to a son, and they will call him Immanuel, which means 'God is with us.'' When Joseph woke up, he did as the angel of the Lord commanded and took Mary as his wife. But he did not have sexual relations with her until her son was born. And Joseph named him Jesus (NLT)."

What can we learn from these events? 1) The angel appeared to Joseph in a dream. 2) We learn that Joseph was a righteous (God-fearing) man. 3) The angel told Joseph, *"Do not be afraid to take Mary as your wife."* 4) The angel provided the baby's name—Jesus. 5) He told Joseph—Jesus' mission —to save us from our sins. 6) The angel said that Jesus' birth would fulfill the prophecy. 7) The angel told Joseph that even the name—Jesus—would proclaim Him as God.

In essence, this encounter gave Joseph much-needed information, direction, and instructions. The angel allayed Joseph's fears (even before they could be formed). And he explained that Jesus would be no ordinary child.

It isn't easy to put ourselves in Joseph's shoes ... but how the angel must have brought peace to such surprising news. And what wonder must have filled his soul to become part of the Messiah's plan for every generation from then to now.

Here's another angelic visitation from Luke 2:13-14. *"Suddenly, the angel was joined by a vast host of others—the armies of heaven—praising God and saying, 'Glory to God in the highest heaven, and peace on earth to those with whom God is pleased (NLT).'"* The lyrics of Angels We Have Heard on High are based on the Bible passage from Luke 2:8-15 from which I've highlighted these key verses.

Dear Lord, thank You for angels, which were part of Your story, and take part in Scripture from Genesis to Revelation of Your Holy Word. Thank You for the ways that they are present in our lives as protection and for the picture they paint in giving You eternal glory. We are grateful for their lessons of instruction, obedience, and adoration. Amen.

Greetings, Favored One!

"Now in the sixth month the angel Gabriel was sent from God to a city in Galilee named Nazareth, to a virgin betrothed to a man whose name was Joseph, of the descendants of David; and the virgin's name was Mary. And coming in, he said to her, 'Greetings, favored one! The Lord is with you.' But she was very perplexed at this statement, and was pondering what kind of greeting this was. And the angel said to her, 'Do not be afraid, Mary, for you have found favor with God. And behold, you will conceive in your womb and give birth to a son, and you shall name Him Jesus. He will be great and will be called the Son of the Most High.'"
Luke 1:26-28 NASB

Dear Lord, this is one of the most beautiful angelic visitations in Your Holy Word. The announcement of Your birth to this tender-aged teen, Mary, brings our hearts delight. Her willingness to obey with such a servant-like attitude is an example that has stood the test of time for all generations. May we be like her in our listening and following and ponder Your goodness and faithfulness as she did (especially in this yuletide season.) And Jesus, may we find favor in Your eyes so that we, too, exalt You as the Most High God. Amen.

At an angel's appearance, Mary's response was to obey. God said this gave her favored status in His sight. Our obedience to the Lord's decrees incurs the same result today.

Good News of Great Joy!

"Shepherds were in the fields near Bethlehem. They were taking turns watching their flock during the night. An angel from the Lord suddenly appeared to them. The glory of the Lord filled the area with light, and they were terrified. The angel said to them, 'Don't be afraid! I have good news for you, a message that will fill everyone with joy.'" Luke 2:8-10 GWT

Dear Jesus, Your birth announcement was indeed Good News that elicited great joy. This was over 2000 years ago, and it still brings our hearts great delight today. I love to picture myself (and encourage others to do the same) by stepping into a scene like this in the Bible.

Simple shepherds were out doing what they usually did —tending their lambs—when suddenly, Your glory descended from heaven. And an angel delivered an audible message—Good News—that a Holy Babe would come wrapped in humanity to dwell among us. Can you imagine the following words ... "Don't be afraid?" It goes against our natural reaction. Right? Yet their hearts must have been filled with wonderment that such a visitation would come to them in the wee hours. Lord, we're grateful for the gift of Your Son—in such a humble package—divinely born and sent to save us from our sins. What a joy it is to celebrate all You've done for us— not just in this Christmas season—but always. Amen.

An angel brought Good News to simple shepherds— Jesus would arrive soon—and His appearance would bring joy to the world and to every heart which receives Him.

The Exultation of our King!

"Adore Him! Give Him praise, you heavenly messengers (angels), you powerful creatures who listen to and act on His every word. Give praise to the Eternal, all armies of heaven—you servants who stand ready to do His will." Psalm 103:20-21 VOICE

Dear Jehovah, I love how this verse summarizes angels as—Your heavenly messengers, servants, and creatures who listen, act, and obey Your Will. They are also depicted as giving You constant praise. What a beautiful image to behold—since You've given us such unique glimpses of their roles in Your Holy Scriptures!

From prophets to comforters, bearers of Your Good News to bring the announcement of Your birth, from displaying how You care for us now, to how they obey Your every command—these wondrous creatures are the blessing of heaven and earth. You've made them to fulfill Your ministry to every heart in some fashion. And while we are instructed to emulate Your life, these angelic qualities—praise, listening, obeying, and serving You align perfectly with what it means to be a Christ-follower. So Lord, let us be a little more like You and them in our attitudes and deeds, we pray. Amen.

....

The example of angels—to praise, serve, listen, and act in obedience to Christ—helps us emulate the life of Jesus day by day until we, too, join the Lord, His saints, and angels in the eternal exultation of our King.

Under the Shadow of the Almighty!

"He who dwells in the secret place of the Most High shall abide under the shadow of the Almighty." (vs. 1) "For He shall give His angels charge over you, to keep you in all your ways." (vs. 11) Psalm 91:1 &11 NKJV

Abba Daddy, these two verses from Psalm 91 have comforted me in many different circumstances. They reassure us that drawing near to You is our safest place. Here we find refuge and rest. We find Your protection and peace. And as the second verse promises that You watch over us, but then, in addition, You also assign angels to keep tabs on us as well. What a careful Guardian You are of us, O Lord. How thankful I am that You never leave or forsake us (Hebrews 13:5). Knowing that You are vigilant in Your faithful observance of my life—keeps me trusting You and helps encourage my belief in greater and greater measures each day. Amen.

....
....
....

Staying close to the presence of God means that He is the Guardian of us and instructs His angels to guard and protect us also. Why would anyone walk this life alone without placing their faith in the Holy One, the Most High God? Is there any area you're withholding from the Lord's care and oversight? The same angels that were present at the manger are also Guardians of every child of God.

I'm Sending an Angel!

"See, I am sending an angel ahead of you to guard you along the way and to bring you to the place I have prepared." Exodus 23:20 NIV

Father God, we were preparing to make a 1000-mile journey to the East Coast when You brought this verse to my attention. As I was praying through it in order to commit it to memory, I noticed that You were providing a number of promises within the words. 1) You are sending an angel to accompany us. 2 Ahead of us. 3) To guard us. 4) Along the way. 5) And to bring us to the place You've prepared.

In other words, God goes with us. He protects the way ahead. He guards and keeps us. And He's bringing us to a "prepared place." This means our current destination, but also our ultimate destination — eternity — as well. The totality of this promise struck me. It sank deeply into my soul and has become an almost daily recitation on my part to cover every area of my life. No matter if we are walking, driving, or biking ... God goes with us. He resides within us. This has brought me such comfort, joy, and peace. Jesus, I thank You for how Your Word speaks encouragement to our minds, hearts, and souls. And I especially praise You for the eternal place — heaven — that You're preparing for those You call Your child. Amen.

How would your life change if you were consciously aware that God sent an angel to go with you wherever you go? Now, you know! Let this truth bring you comfort and peace. Trust God with every step of your journey.

Ministering Spirits

"Are not all the angels ministering spirits sent out [by God] to serve (accompany, protect) those who will inherit salvation? [Of course they are!]" Hebrews 1:14 AMP

Dear Heavenly Father, there is something so wondrous about the idea of angels acting as ministering spirits. These holy beings act on Your behalf and participate in the work of the saving grace which You make available to all people.

They serve You, protect Your children, and move in tandem with the Spirit to bring about the redemption of a heart that calls upon Your name. What a blessed duty this must be. How the angels must rejoice as the rolls of heaven increase daily. And how they must bow in worship at Your Holy throne to esteem You as King of Kings. Lord, I bow too, in awe of Who You are and that I am a soul whose name is written in the Lamb's Book of Life. It may be an undeserved gift, but Jesus, my appreciation knows no end! Amen.

<u>Pause in the Word</u>: *Please look up and read 1 Kings 19:1-9. Make a few observations about how an angel encouraged Elijah.*

Angels serve and protect us in tandem with the Spirit— so that we can answer Christ's whisper within our hearts—to make our most important decision by making Him Lord of all.

The Lord Delivers!

"The angel of the Lord encamps around those who fear him, and he delivers them." Psalm 34:7 NIV

Father God, this verse may be short, but it's also sweet. It's an affirmation of Your affection, protection, and deliverance. It's a reminder that You care for those who seek You and obey Your Word. And since encamp — means to encircle, surround, or guard on all sides — it gives us a word picture of Your faithful care being provided by Your guardians — angels.

Lord, I give You honor and pray that my life brings You glory. I bow before You and cannot adequately express my gratitude for Who You are to me and the work that You're doing through me. I encamp in Your presence daily, Jesus, and ask for Your Guardianship in every area of my life. Amen

Pause in the Word: Please look up Psalm 46:1, Psalm 32:7, and Psalm 17:8. How do these promises bring you assurance? Jot down your insights and give thanks to God for what He reveals.

....

....

....

....

Revere the Lord, give Him Your highest praise and first priority, and He'll send angels to encamp 'round your life as a sign of His affection and deliverance.

Celebrate with me!

"Imagine a woman who has ten coins and loses one. Won't she light a lamp and scour the house, looking in every nook and cranny until she finds it? And when she finds it you can be sure she'll call her friends and neighbors: 'Celebrate with me! I found my lost coin!' Count on it—that's the kind of party God's angels throw whenever one lost soul turns to God." Luke 15:10 MSG

Dear Jesus, Luke 15 gives us a couple of examples in a row of a lost soul turning to You—for forgiveness, mercy, grace, and the gift of Salvation. Verses 4-7 use the parable of a shepherd who would leave 99 sheep to find one who had wandered off. In verse 10, You illustrate the same point using a woman who loses one of 10 coins and celebrates when it is found. This is again likened to one soul who comes into Your kingdom. How beautiful it is to picture (in our minds) the angel's rejoicing as we come to know You as our personal Savior. How amazing to envision heaven's praise as it occurs over and over all across the globe. And how precious to think that when You gave Your life upon a tree at Calvary—that You gave us the greatest offering of love—that could have ever been poured out to give us eternity with You and the angels forever. That's a reason to celebrate—today and every day! And Abba Daddy, I do! Amen.

For every life that comes to Christ—like a child—the Lamb of God throws an angelic party in heaven to welcome them into the family of God. Don't miss yours!

The

FIRST

Noel

A Meditation on The First Noel

The first Noel was the greeting to the shepherds who were tending their flocks in the field. Under a velvet sky lit with sparkling stars, they received an angelic announcement of the Christ-child's birth. Immediately, they gathered their flocks and went swiftly to where the star shone like a beacon to illumine their path. And then, imagine the wonder that filled their souls at finding Jesus—just as had been predicted. The first living nativity came to life—giving the world notice—that the Savior had arrived.

I'm sure at some point, you've either sent a birth announcement for your child or received one to celebrate someone else's newborn babe. Having this kind of notice arrive in the mailbox is always sweet. Joy fills our hearts for those to whom this fantastic event is about to unfold. And I can only imagine how the Bible characters reacted as the news of Jesus' arrival struck them as they got word or attended Him at the manger.

Some fell on their faces at the news. Some traveled to find Him. Others brought gifts of adoration and worship. Some immediately rejoiced. Some pondered and experienced awe. And many felt gratitude as His mission and ministry would become clear throughout time and the telling of His Word.

Galatians 4:4-7 gives us a look back at these events. I found this an interesting perspective from which to view the nativity. *"When the right time arrived, God sent His Son into this world (born of a woman, subject to the law) to free those who, just like Him, were subject to the law. Ultimately He wanted us all to be adopted as sons and daughters. Because you are now part of God's family, He sent the Spirit of His Son into our hearts; and the Spirit calls out, 'Abba, Father.' You no longer have to live as a slave because you are a child of God. And since you are His child, God guarantees an inheritance is waiting for you (VOICE)."*

We're invited to the manager via a reflective lens that displays: 1) Jesus came to free us. 2) He has adopted us. 3) He calls us sons and daughters. 4) We are considered part of His family (if we have received Him as Lord by faith). 5) His Spirit indwells our hearts. 6) We are no longer slaves but heirs. 7) God gives us eternal life as an inheritance.

Dear Jesus, thank You that the predictions of Your birth (from Isaiah and the angelic visitations) all came true. Thank You for coming to earth as a Babe to take away the world's sins. And thank You for living out that mission at age 33 upon the Cross of Calvary. I am grateful to be called one of Your own. I worship You as the Christ-child. I adore You as the Son Who made a way for all to be saved. And I praise You for Your Spirit, Who lives in my heart to help me obey Your Word and Will. Help me, Lord, to live as an announcement of Your love, grace, and joy daily. Let that first Noel be my anthem and my song unto Your throne. Amen.

Read the Word from John 1 (below), then compare it to Galatians 4. Think about how these passages compare or contrast.

John 1:9-14 & 29-31 TLB. The one who is the true Light arrived to shine on everyone coming into the world. But although he made the world, the world didn't recognize him when he came. Even in his own land and among his own people, the Jews, he was not accepted. Only a few would welcome and receive him. But to all who received him, he gave the right to become children of God. All they needed to do was to trust him to save them. All those who believe this are reborn! —not a physical rebirth resulting from human passion or plan—but from the will of God. And Christ became a human being and lived here on earth among us and was full of loving forgiveness and truth. And some of us have seen his glory—the glory of the only Son of the heavenly Father! ... The next day John saw Jesus coming toward him and said, 'Look! There is the Lamb of God who takes away the world's sin! He is the one I was talking about when I said, 'Soon a man far greater than I am is coming, who existed long before me!' I didn't know he was the one, but I am here baptizing with water in order to point him out to the nation of Israel.'"

Celebrate Jesus' Birth!

"So Joseph also went up from the town of Nazareth in Galilee to Judea, to Bethlehem the town of David, because he belonged to the house and line of David. He went there to register with Mary, who was pledged to be married to him and was expecting a child. While they were there, the time came for the baby to be born, and she gave birth to her firstborn, a son. She wrapped him in cloths and placed him in a manger because there was no place for them in the inn." Luke 2:4-7 NIV

Dear Jesus, Yours is the sweetest birth announcement in all of history. This one—telling of Your impending arrival—has melted many a heart. It paved the way for You to reach all mankind with Your love. While it may not have been printed and engraved on some beautiful stationery—it was an invitation to know You and Your grace—which was later written with Your precious blood. While You were wrapped in swaddling clothes at the manger, You would later be stripped and beaten at the Cross. And while there was no room at the inn, You came to dwell in every heart that makes room in their lives to call You Lord.

We are grateful, Lord Christ. We are thankful to be part of Your lineage, called heirs, and one day—citizens of heaven. Amen.

The birth of Jesus made our spiritual rebirth possible. What a gift You are to our world, Jesus, and to our hearts.

The Good News was Delivered!

"The angel said, 'Don't be afraid. I'm here to announce a great and joyful event that is meant for everybody, worldwide.'" Luke 2:10 MSG See also Matthew 24:14.

Father God, one of the blessings of the Christmas season is that joy seems to fill the air. Carols are playing on the radio, in shops, and sung in our churches. There's a sense of celebration—for Your birth and to be shared from our hearts, homes, and pantries. I love these verses from Luke and Matthew, which proclaim Your Good News—not just to the little town of Bethlehem—not simply to the region where You were born—but, instead, to the entire world. And I love that Your Gospel will be preached this way before You return. Your invitation, and Your heart's desire, is that no one would be separated from You (or perish—John 3:16-17).

You want everyone to hear the good tidings of Your love, grace, forgiveness, and mercy. You want every man, woman, boy, and girl to experience You as Lord and understand that You died, were baptized, and rose again to reign on high. And You want every single person ever born to receive the gift of Salvation—eternity in Your presence. That's the message You came to share; it's the message of hope that is the spirit of Christmas. Amen.

Jesus was born over 2000 years ago to bring Good News to the world. He gave His life to make this news become the Gospel Truth. And that message is going 'round the world to share His love. Has this joy reached your soul?

The Firstborn of all Creation!

"He is the image of the invisible God, the firstborn of all creation: for by Him all things were created, both in the heavens and on earth, visible and invisible, whether thrones, or dominions, or rulers, or authorities—all things have been created through Him and for Him. He is before all things, and in Him all things hold together." Colossians 1:15-17 NASB

Dear Jesus, these verses from Colossians tell us that You are the "firstborn of Creation." They call You Creator. They explain that You have dominion over the visible and invisible realms, powers, and every type of spirit. All things were created by You, through You, and for Your glory. You are above all things and hold them together by Your hand. These words display Your power, sovereignty, holiness, and omnipotence. They leave me feeling humble and in awe of Your majesty. You existed before all things and are infinite. Each of these attributes means that we can trust You and rely upon You. They suggest that every blessing that we enjoy flows from Your loving kindness. And they mean You are One with the Father and the Holy Spirit. I bow before You, O God because there is none like You. Worthy are You to receive all our praise. Amen.

If you have a high and holy view of God, a reverent fear and love for Him, He'll invite You into an intimate relationship. Then you'll learn to know Him as Abba Daddy, Friend, Comforter, Guardian, and the One to Whom you can turn for your every need.

New Birth & New Life

"When God our Savior revealed his kindness and love, he saved us, not because of the righteous things we had done, but because of his mercy. He washed away our sins, giving us a new birth and new life through the Holy Spirit. He generously poured out the Spirit upon us through Jesus Christ our Savior. Because of his grace he made us right in his sight and gave us confidence that we will inherit eternal life." Titus 3:4-7 NLT

Dear Jesus, I remember the evening I gave my heart to You as a little girl. Two guest speakers visited our church, and they brought Your Word to life via songs, puppets, and artwork. This approach made You real to my young heart. I wanted to know You. I wanted You to be Lord over my life, every decision, and my every step. Through the years, I began to memorize Scripture and understood more and more what Your gift meant to me. Thus, I wanted to share Who You are with others. I continue to look back over childhood and see Your hand of protection, Your Spirit's guidance, and how You blessed this child who cried out to You. Lord, thank You for making me right in Your sight—then and now. Thank You for hearing my every plea, confession, and praise. And thank You for walking me through every step of this life. Because as I continue to run this race— it's still my desire to share Who You are—with my world in ways that make You real to others because my contagious joy cannot be contained! Amen.

How can you make God's Word and His truths come alive to someone today?

God is Working in You!

"For I am not ashamed of this Good News about Christ. It is the power of God at work, saving everyone who believes—the Jew first and also the Gentile." Romans 1:16 NLT

Dear Lord, I pray for greater courage daily to proclaim Your Good News. I ask that You strengthen my resolve to love others as You do. Fill me with Your grace and words to defend Your Gospel message. Jesus, help me stand upon Your truth and to have a heart of love.

Grant me a fresh filling of Your Spirit to obey Your Word and Your Will for my life. And give me a heart of kindness—even if others come against me for my faith in You. It's my desire to please You and represent You well as Your child. Amen.

"For God is working in you, giving you the desire and the power to do what pleases him." Philippians 2:13 NLT

<u>Pause in the Word</u>: Please look up Isaiah 50:7 and Psalm 25:20, particularly in the NASB translations. How do these relate to Romans 1:16 and Philippians 2:13?

Jesus' saving work at the Cross means that He's at work within the heart and life of every Christ-follower to enable us to carry out the mission of sharing His Good News.

The Living and Everlasting Word of God!

"Now that you have obeyed the truth and have purified your souls to love your brothers sincerely, you must love one another intensely and with a pure heart. For you have been born again, not by a seed that perishes but by one that cannot perish—by the living and everlasting word of God. For 'All human life is like grass, and all its glory is like a flower in the grass. The grass dries up and the flower drops off, but the word of the Lord lasts forever.' Now this word is the good news that was announced to you." 1 Peter 1:22-25 ISV

Dear Lord, I love these verses from 1 Peter, which use rich imagery from creation to assure us of Your eternal Word, presence, and Salvation. From seed to flower—these things which are described as temporary and perishing—are contrasted by Your steadfast nature and love for us. You encourage us to share what You're developing within us with others. And You're teaching us that to share the Good News that we've been given means that we will leave behind a legacy of faith from one generation to the next. That's how we will be obedient. That's how Your love will shine through us. That's how we'll demonstrate our love for You and give You honor and glory. Though our days are fleeting, O God, may we live each one with gratitude and hearts that serve You wholeheartedly. Amen.

How can you be more effective at focusing on the imperishable—so that those around you do not perish?

The Wonderful Grace of God!

"My life is worth nothing to me unless I use it for finishing the work assigned me by the Lord Jesus—the work of telling others the Good News about the wonderful grace of God." Acts 20:24 NLT

Dear Jesus, Philippians 1:6 tells us this: *"I am sure that God who began the good work within you will keep right on helping you grow in his grace until his task within you is finally finished on that day when Jesus Christ returns."* **These verses encourage our hearts to work heartily unto You each day. They teach us that You are to be our priority. Nothing we do is more important than loving You and others—so much so—that we want to pave the way for our friends and family to be part of Your family. Your grace is a precious gift. It came at the cost of Your life upon Calvary. And You purchased our freedom by redeeming us so that we are not eternally separated from You.**

How I need You, Jesus! And how thankful I am to use my life to plant seeds for Your kingdom. Without You, I am nothing. Help me to run my race with Your Spirit's guidance, wisdom, joy, and empowerment, I pray. And let praise be the exaltation of my heart unto You. Amen.

The only thing I have to boast about is the cause of Christ. Because He's forgiven me and calls me His child —I want others to experience this expensive, lavish grace—so that you, too, can know Him and share this Good News!

Sing to the Lord!

"Sing a new song to the Lord! Sing to the Lord, all the world! Sing to the Lord, and praise him! Proclaim every day the good news that he has saved us. Proclaim his glory to the nations, his mighty deeds to all peoples."
Psalm 96:1-3 GNT

Heavenly Father, how I love to sing Your praises. Whether it's a hymn, a beloved carol—such as the First Noel, O Holy Night, or What Child is This? or a chorus— my heart beats faster to exalt You. Christmas is such a beautiful time of year. It's the perfect time to proclaim You as King, Messiah, and Emmanuel. It's a wonderful time to share our faith and what You're doing in our lives. And it's a precious time to share the story of Your birth and the hope that we have in You. Thank You, Jesus, for coming as a humble Babe to ordinary people like shepherds. Thank You for using a young couple as servants. And thank You for using creation—a star and angels—to point to Your holiness. We are filled with awe at Your love for us. We long to give You the honor and praise that You deserve. And we want the whole world to know and celebrate You as their King. Amen.

....
....

What's your favorite carol or hymn? Why does it speak to your heart? How does it proclaim God's glory? If you could write a chorus—what words would you choose to exalt Jesus—as the Babe, Messiah, and Emmanuel?

Do You Hear what I HEAR?

A Meditation on Do You Hear What I Hear?

Do You Hear What I Hear? has been a favorite carol of mine since I was a child. I always loved that this title forms a question with lyrics that supply Spiritual and whimsical answers.

In this section, we'll explore how Jesus' birth was announced, the angel's promise of peace to its recipients, and how joy permeated the hearts of those who sought and found the Christ-child. But here in this study, we'll look at what God's Word tells us about our questions, Jesus' questions, and the answers only the Father can supply.

First of all, I cherish the promise of Matthew 7:7-8 that we are invited to bring any inquiry to the Lord. And He makes us a few promises. Let's take a look. *"Ask and it will be given to you; seek and you will find; knock and the door will be opened to you. For everyone who asks receives; the one who seeks finds; and to the one who knocks, the door will be opened."* Of note? The NLT translation uses the following language: *"Keep on asking ... keep on seeking ... and keep on knocking."* This means that we are to have faith in what we ask for but to enter into a persistent type of prayer—which means that we are continually seeking a relationship with Christ. This attitude is vital to know God and understand His ways.

Let's look at a few more truths from His holy Word: Romans 10:17 tells us: *"So faith comes from hearing, that is, hearing the Good News about Christ (NLT)."* Luke 11:28 says, *"But Jesus said, 'Those who hear the teaching of God and obey it—they are the ones who are truly blessed (ICB).'"* Matthew 13:23 tells us, *"And the one on whom seed was sown on the good soil, this is the man who hears the word and understands it; who indeed bears fruit and brings forth, some a hundredfold, some sixty, and some thirty (NASB)."*

Notice anything? 1) We must hear the Word of God. 2) We must obey it. 3) We only bear the fruit of His Spirit by applying His truths and promises. 4) To do any of these ... we often have questions ... that the Lord welcomes and promises to answer.

Where did Jesus go when He had questions? To the Father. Throughout Scripture, we find Jesus seeking solitude in a posture of prayer (See Mark 1:35, Luke 6:12-13). He wrestled with the Father's Will, just as we sometimes do. (See the scene of Gethsemane in Matthew 26). While He was fully divine, Jesus was also fully human. He got tired. He experienced emotional pain as we do. (See John 11). And while I could cite numerous other examples, I'll give you one more: Jesus forgave others—just as we need to—and did so right up to the moment of His death on the Cross. (See Luke 23:34).

We have many questions in life. As soon as we learn to speak, we begin to form them. God instilled within us a sense of curiosity. This enables us to learn, explore, grow, invent, and process information. And I've learned that the Lord is very patient with questions focused on understanding Him, His ways, or His Word.

The key? Be ready to apply what He speaks into your heart. Listen carefully. Do you hear what I hear? God's been trying to tell you to call upon His name, to come and give Him praise, and to seek His company. What will He do? He'll meet you right where you are. Provide for you. And either give you an answer or draw you so close to His side that you are perfectly content to wait in His presence and know He is God. He is in control. And that in Him, you can experience a peace that echoes like a carol in the breeze.

Look up the verses in parenthesis from above, then jot down what you hear. Did one of these topics resonate in your heart? Seeking the Father in solitude? Wrestling with the Spirit to obey God's Will? The need to forgive? What about the area of being content? Or how about praising God at all times? (See 1 Thessalonians 5:16-18).

Call Him Immanuel!

"Therefore the Lord himself will give you a sign: The virgin will conceive and give birth to a son, and will call him Immanuel." Isaiah 7:14 ESV

Father God, I cherish the places in Scripture with the word "therefore." It indicates to us that we are about to hear precise information or detailed instructions or some messianic promise. And in this case, the news that You are giving is three-fold: 1) You would provide a "sign," and 2) That sign—would come through the divine birth of Your precious Son, Jesus. The third part of the promise is that You would be called Emmanuel, meaning "God with us" or "God saves us." And that is precisely why You came to earth wrapped in humanity. Lord, thank You for being Emmanuel—God within us—and God with us (amid all circumstances). You are the One we need to save us from our sins, to bring us joy, peace, hope, and deliverance. And we long to give You the place of honor that You deserve—a home in our hearts—room in our souls to dwell. Teach us to be attuned to Your voice, Your messages, and the beautiful ways You communicate that You're near. Amen.

....
....

There was no room in the inn, yet the irony? Jesus is called Emmanuel—God with us—because He has room for every heart for everyone that answers His invitation to call upon His name to be saved! And He, in turn, makes His home in us—forever.

Joy

His Roots shall bear Fruit!

"There shall come forth a shoot from the stump of Jesse, and a branch from his roots shall bear fruit. And the Spirit of the Lord shall rest upon him, the Spirit of wisdom and understanding, the Spirit of counsel and might, the Spirit of knowledge and the fear of the Lord. And his delight shall be in the fear of the Lord."
Isaiah 11:1-3 ESV

Lord God, these prophetic words, which use a tree as imagery, are so profound to Your journey. Here You're compared—the coming Christ-child—as a branch from roots that will bear fruit. In John 15:5, we're told, *"I am the vine; you are the branches."* Jeremiah 17:7-8 describes a life grafted into You—like a tree with deep roots that flourish beside the water's edge that is leafy, healthy, and produces fruit. And upon a tree, forged of two beams—a Cross—You gave Your life for all mankind. How the Spirit rested upon Your life. And how You delighted Him with Your every miracle, healing, and act of kindness! We are so grateful for every gift from Your life and example. And while we often miss the mark, Jesus, we delight in You and are thankful for the love You demonstrated from the manger to the Cross and beyond. Amen.

Jesus is described as coming from a "shoot from the stump of Jesse"—as a means of tracing His genealogy. He's called a branch and shown the favor of God. And the Father takes great delight in Jesus' ministry of love —from creation to birth to death to resurrection— because He is holy, He keeps His Word, and His promises and divine dynasty are everlasting.

He will be Great!

"Do not be afraid, Mary, for you have found favor with God. And behold, you will conceive in your womb and bear a son, and you shall call his name Jesus. He will be great and will be called the Son of the Most High. And the Lord God will give to him the throne ... and he will reign over the house of Jacob forever, and of his kingdom there will be no end." Luke 1:29-33 ESV

Dear Lord, I can only imagine Mary's initial reaction when an angel appeared to her in the night with this verbal greeting. Most of us would have responded with fear, trembling, and a sense of awe. Then, to have Your holy messenger deliver words—of favor, of a divine mission, and to be granted a place in Your lineage that serves as her testimony! I love how she pondered every piece of the story You were unfolding and how she had a willing and obedient heart to be Your servant. To give birth to a perfect child, the Son of God, and to be given the promise that He will be a gift to all mankind ... her mind must not have been able to absorb it all. Yet, this unlikely tender-aged teen who was pure of mind, body, and soul became the instrument of Your choosing to bring the blessing of the Christ-child into Your world and our hearts. Thank You, Lord, for favoring us with this precious gift. Amen.

Mary may have considered herself an unlikely or unworthy choice to bear the Son of God—yet she believed and acted on what she heard. In what area do you see the Lord using your weakness or unworthiness —for His glory?

Of the Royal Line of David!

"For the Scriptures clearly state that the Messiah will be born of the royal line of David, in Bethlehem, the village where King David was born." John 7:42 NLT

Dear Jesus, You were born in the little town of Bethlehem. This humble place held Your cradle. Its dirt streets were traversed by You, Mary, and Joseph—to arrive at an inn within the city's walls. It bespoke a heritage of Your lineage. And this small village, with only a manger to offer, became the first place You would lay Your head, be held, and loved. I wonder how the generations who came before You felt as they learned about Your birth. Did they celebrate the coming Messiah, the Christ-child, and King of Kings as arriving in the place where they live(d)? Did they give You honor and worship? Or did they doubt that such a place could be where the Savior of the world would arrive? Did they listen and learn from You, Your Word, and ways? For to me, Abba Daddy, I treasure Your humility. I cherish that while You were fully divine, You were also wrapped in humanity and embraced us as Your children, part of Your eternal family. Amen.

The little town of Bethlehem became a precious place on a map because it's where Jesus was born. Many would come before Him to proclaim Him as Messiah. Many continue to come after Him to proclaim Him as Savior. Many more will enter into a new city to live in His presence for all time! Have you heard the Good News, which first came to a small village called Bethlehem?

Come and Worship!

"Where is He who has been born King of the Jews? For we saw His star in the east and have come to worship Him." Matthew 2:2 NKJV

Dear Christ-child, I cherish how the shepherds and wise men began to seek You. They came with a question. They came with a sense of expectation. They came to find, to be answered, and followed the sign that You provided. They also came with hearts that longed to know You personally and intimately and to give You praise and worship. Sometimes things happen in life ... and we tend to ask ... "Where is He?" "Where is God when _____ occurs?" The answer is the same today as it was then: to the one who asks, You answer.

The one who seeks will find. And the one who follows will be given signposts of Your presence within our hearts and right beside us for every step of our journey! Jesus, we come to worship You too! And while the wise men followed an earthly star—we seek You, Lord, as the Bright and Morning Star—because forever, You reign. Amen.

....

....

Matthew 7:7-8 tells us to ask, seek, and knock. A few translations encourage these three actions to be repeated often in pursuing the Lord. He welcomes every inquiry on our part—because it means that we are drawing near, are listening for His guidance, and have the heart to obey Him.

Magnify the Lord with Me!

"And Mary said, 'My soul magnifies and exalts the Lord, and my spirit has rejoiced in God my Savior. For He has looked [with loving care] on the humble state of His maidservant; for behold, ... generations will count me blessed and happy and favored by God! For He who is mighty has done great things for me; and holy is His name [to be worshiped in His purity, majesty, and glory].'" Luke 1:46-49 AMP

Dear Lord, was "Mary's song" one of the most lovely voices You heard around Your throne? Has anyone's praise ever rivaled hers for its clarity and joy-filled response to following Your Will? Can we mirror her heart of love for You, Jesus? Can we be like the woman who brought her alabaster jar to anoint You—out of devotion? Will You teach us to be a reflection of this type of holy, unabashed willingness to unashamedly pour out our hearts in gratitude for Who You are to us? Father, that's our prayer. That's our heart's desire. And that's the echo of our souls this Christmas season.

We exalt You! We are blessed to sit at Your feet, hear Your voice, talk to You, and be taught from Your Word. Oh, Jesus, we are favored to keep company with You, to worship You and experience Your faithful care. Amen.

God looks on us as He did on Mary ... with favor, blessing, love ... when we show Him that we hold Him in the highest esteem. Have we shown appreciation and honored His holy name lately? He'd love to hear your voice raised in song!

To Treasure!

"When they had seen him, they spread the word concerning what had been told them about this child, and all who heard it were amazed at what the shepherds said to them. But Mary treasured up all these things and pondered them in her heart. The shepherds returned, glorifying and praising God for all the things they had heard and seen, which were just as they had been told." Luke 2:17-20 NIV

Dear Jesus, it must have been amazing to be one of the shepherds to whom the angels announced Your birth. It's no wonder word spread concerning these miraculous events. Yours was the arrival of a King, a delivery set apart from all that would come before or after. And it's no wonder Your earthly mother, Mary, was filled with contemplation at all that happened, all that You promised and brought to pass. I'm sure she experienced many emotions, from joy to confusion, to awe at being chosen for this unique role. I'm sure she joined with the shepherds in singing and glorifying Your name. As You brought each prophecy to pass, You confirmed Your love, Your mission and that everything told to these Biblical characters was true because that is Who You are. And we long to spread this Good News, Lord, for You are our treasure! Amen.

....
....

Pondering and praising are so closely related that you must take the action of the first to offer the Lord the second. Then, we have something to share, indeed!

He Calls us Sons and Daughters!

"But when the set time had fully come, God sent his son, born of a woman, born under the law, to redeem those under the law, that we might receive adoption to sons/daughters. Because you are his sons/daughters, God sent the Spirit of His Son into our hearts, the who calls out, Abba, Father." Galatians 4:4-5 NIV

Holy Father, thank You for the Baby Jesus, born of flesh (Mary), and Your Holy Spirit to bring us redemption. We are so blessed to be adopted into Your family as sons and daughters. Thank You for filling us with Your Spirit and for making Your home in our hearts. We call out to You for our every need. We cry out with our deepest hurts and longings. And we are so thankful for the gift of Salvation, for Your eternal presence that meets us where we are each day.

We treasure being called one of Your own. This privileged position gives us an inheritance that You freely offer because You laid down Your life for us. I'm a grateful soul who calls You, Daddy, Prince of Peace, and the Love of my life. You are my dearest and greatest gift. Amen.

We are called sons and daughters if we've asked Jesus to be the Lord of our lives. Call upon Him today—for your greatest need, to offer praise, and for His Spirit's guidance in your life. Then rest in your inheritance— adoption—being fully known and loved because you are!

Joy to the World...

A Meditation on
Joy to the World

If you are a man—imagine how you might have felt if you were Adam when God presented him with the first woman. His jaw may have dropped, a huge smile lit his face, and he may have expressed joy at the miracle God had formed—from his rib. If you're a woman, imagine your favorite scene from the Garden of Eden—the perfect setting, a sweet breeze filling the air, the birdsong filling the trees, the varied hues and scents of every flower in perfectly formed flowerbeds without thorny weeds. Doesn't it fill you with a sense of joy?

Now imagine yourself in the field tending your flock of lambs and having angels appear with a greeting of joy—delivered especially for them—but also "for all people" and for every generation that would follow. Think about the wonder that must have filled their souls! Does picturing it—evoke a similar spiritual emotion in yours?

Now think of a time in your life that brought you a deep sense of joy. Was it good news that you received? A special gift? The day you were married or when you had your first child? Was it the day that you accepted Christ as your Savior? Was it when you realized that Salvation meant that you'll spend eternity with Jesus? I hope the spiritual ideas from this list have lit your soul with delight and anticipation.

I love the places in God's holy Word that speak of what joy is, what it does for us, and how it's a contagious emotion to be shared.

Let's look at a few verses that reflect these truths.

- Nehemiah 8:10 tells us, *"The joy of the Lord is your strength (NIV)."*
- Psalm 119:111 says, *"Your statues are my heritage forever; they are the joy of my heart (NIV)."*
- Proverbs 17:22 reminds us *"that a joyful heart is good medicine (ESV)."*
- Psalm 47:1 instructs us: *"Clap your hands, all you nations; shout to God with cries of joy (NIV)."*
- Malachi 4:2 provides a promise: *"But unto you who revere and worshipfully fear My name shall the Sun of Righteousness arise with healing in His wings and His beams, and you shall go forth and gambol like calves {released} from the stall and leap for joy."* AMPC

Notice the running theme? Whether joy comes from God's Word or His Spirit—it brings about change, healing, and praise and gives us a proper sense (or perspective) of Who the Lord is. I treasure the places in Scripture that relate joy to creation—as being boundless—(See Isaiah 55:12 and Psalm 98:8).

Here's some space to unpack a few of your thoughts of joy.

....
....
....

I encourage you to read Isaiah 35. Notice how joy is used in this passage and what joy yields. Then jot down your discoveries.

....
....
....
....

News that will Affect all People!

(Angelic) Messenger: "Don't be afraid! Listen! I bring good news, news of great joy, news that will affect all people everywhere." Luke 2:10 VOICE

Dear Lord, I love to imagine myself in the scenes of the Bible. This has helped me grow and to understand more of Your ways. It has made Your Holy Scriptures come alive and has helped me meditate upon Your goodness. It has been a way that I've learned to put "myself in someone's shoes," whether to understand their fear or doubt, to gain courage, more faith, or see that Bible characters had flaws too. This verse tells us that an angel —one of Your heavenly messengers came to earth— telling the shepherds in the field not to be afraid, to listen up—that he brought good tidings—not only for them but for us too. Your impending arrival would change the course of the world. It would shake and shape the foundation of our faith. And You would become the Way, Truth, and Life—the path to Salvation. One tiny Baby would be born in Bethlehem, and nothing would ever be the same. Great joy was coming via an infant's first breath and exhale of life. And the breath of Your Spirit now lives in me—this news affects me every day and makes me want to share the gift that You've given me—everywhere! May I be Your messenger of this Good News to my world too! Amen.

The Good News of Jesus' arrival brought great joy to the hearts of humble shepherds. It still affects surrendered hearts that way today. If you've received this precious gift, are you sharing it with others?

The Glory of the One and only Son!

"The Word became flesh and made his dwelling among us. We have seen his glory, the glory of the one and only Son, who came from the Father, full of grace and truth." John 1:14 NIV

Dear Jesus, while the word "joy" does not appear in this verse, every time I read it, that's what I feel. Thank You, Jesus, for coming to earth as a babe wrapped in humanity. Thank You for coming to live among us on earth and within our hearts as Lord. It brings me such delight to get to know You through Your Word, meditation, prayer, and abiding in Your company.

Thank You for teaching us, reaching out to us, and drawing near to us daily. We long to sink Your promises into our minds and hearts, so we obey You and bring You honor through how we live. Amen.

<u>Pause in the Word</u>: Please look up Psalm 119:105, Luke 11:28, Isaiah 40:8, Psalm 18:30, and Matthew 24:35. Make note of your observations about "the Word" (the Bible), then about Jesus (as the Person and Title from John 1:14) "The Word."

....
....
....

Jesus set aside the glory of heaven—to be wrapped in a cloak of humanity—so that mankind could see Him in all His divinity, splendor, and majesty.

God's precepts give Joy to the Heart!

"The law of the Lord is perfect, refreshing the soul. The statutes of the Lord are trustworthy, making wise the simple. The precepts of the Lord are right, giving joy to the heart. The commands of the Lord are radiant, giving light to the eyes." Psalm 19:7-8 NIV

Father God, thank You for Your Word, which feeds us, encourages, corrects, instructs, and blesses our lives. Your parables and truths teach us how to emulate Your footsteps and show You to be a Promise-keeper. Thank You for Your Spirit, which brings understanding to our minds so we can obey You.

Thank You for Your loyal love that is kind and generous and fills our hearts with joy. Your Holy Scriptures invite us into Your presence. It inspires our faith to grow. It challenges us to lay down our sins, repent, and accept Your covering of grace and forgiveness. It refreshes us like a morning shower on tender plants. And it's with adoration that we lift our faces toward Yours to see a twinkle in our Daddy's eyes when we seek to walk in Your Will. Amen.

"Jesus answered, 'It is written: 'Man shall not live on bread alone, but on every word that comes from the mouth of God.'" Matthew 4:4 NIV

One of the ways that we display our love for God—is by loving His Word, absorbing His truths like a child, then maturing in the faith that we profess.

Complete Joy!

"As the Father has loved me, so have I loved you. Now remain in my love. If you keep my commands, you will remain in my love, just as I have kept my Father's commands and remain in his love. I have told you this so that my joy may be in you and that your joy may be complete (full)." John 15:11 NIV

Dear Jesus, the love of the Father for You is complete, full, and all-encompassing. That's the same kind of love that You demonstrate for us. What a beautiful picture of kindness and wholeness it paints in our souls. You ask us to abide in You, remain in You, in Your love, and keep Your commandments. You're asking us to obey Your Word as a sign of our love for You. You're telling us exactly what to do that will bring You joy and what will make us complete—full—filled with Your Spirit and keep us in perfect communion with You.

Lord, help us love You as You love the Father. Help us listen and put into practice what we learn from Your Scripture. Inscribe these truths and promises into our hearts and minds so that we pass them to future generations, we pray. Amen.

....

....

Jesus showed His love for us by laying down His life for us at Calvary. He's allowing us to demonstrate our love for Him by simply living out the truth of the Good News to the world around us. There's no better way to give Him honor.

The Lord is my Strength and Song!

"Behold, God, my salvation! I will trust and not be afraid, for the Lord God is my strength and song; yes, He has become my salvation. Therefore with joy you will draw water from the springs of salvation. And in that day you will say, 'Give thanks to the Lord, call on His name [in prayer]. Make His deeds known among the peoples [of the earth]; proclaim [to them] that His name is exalted!'" Isaiah 12:1-4 AMP

Jehovah, the Christmas season is a time of joy. It's a time of gatherings, church, and community events; all centered around celebrating Your birth, Jesus. It's a lovely time for lights in every hue to decorate houses, shops, and every street corner. It's a time to share cards, gifts, and Your love. But it can also bring anxiety and exhaustion and leave us drained from all the activity. If that's where you are today ... this verse is for you. Imagine yourself before a well. Now think of yourself lowering a bucket or pitcher down—until it's filled with pure, sparkling, refreshing water. That's what Jesus has to offer you—strength, hope, joy, and peace—so that you can give, bake, and be His vessel of Living water and an outpouring of His gift of Salvation. Christmas should bring out the best in us as a Christ-follower. But for this to be so—we must take time to be in His Word and commune in His presence. Then, we'll have much to share and reasons to proclaim our praise to You, Jesus, with contagious joy. Amen.

Salvation is a gift to us. Let joy overflow from you so that your faith, peace, and hope are contagious this Christmas season, and then give God all the praise.

He will Exult over you with Singing!

"Yahweh your God is in your midst; a mighty warrior who saves. He shall rejoice over you with joy; he renews you in his love; he will exult over you with singing." Zephaniah 3:17 LEB

Father God, I love the idea of You singing over us, especially at Christmastime. Think of it ... just as angels sang manger-side, the Lord sings over you and me to give us hope, joy, encouragement, and peace. What a beautiful image this portrays. The Lord is in our midst—He is present in our circumstances, churches, and families. But He is also present "in our midst"—He lives within our hearts—if we are His child. This truth has brought me such comfort and peace. It fills my soul with elation and adoration for my Savior.

This Warrior—Who gave His life for us—renews, quiets, and transforms us—from the inside out. He is filled with praise at the wonder of His creation—you. And He rejoices when we walk closely with Him, desiring to know more of Him and His ways. O Lord, we are grateful for Your ever-present presence and never-ending love for us. We bring You praise and listen for the echo of Your song of love. Amen.

....
....
....

Sing praise unto the Lord and listen for His echo of rejoicing over whom He's created you to be. Then, live your life unto Him—to the fullest.

Overflowing with Abundance

"The whole earth is filled with awe at your wonders; where morning dawns, where evening fades, you call forth songs of joy. You care for the land and water it; you enrich it abundantly. ... You drench its furrows and level its ridges; you soften it with showers and bless its crops. You crown the year with your bounty, and your carts overflow with abundance. The grasslands of the wilderness overflow; the hills are clothed with gladness. The meadows are covered with flocks and the valleys are mantled with grain; they shout for joy and sing." Psalm 65:8 NIV

Dear Jesus, I treasure images such as this that illustrate "joy" through creation, through Your love for all that You fashioned in the Genesis 1-2 account. You send the dawn to brighten our days. You give showers to produce plants, flowers, and food. You made animals to graze, birds to sing, and have clothed the meadows with wildflowers in abundant and vibrant shades. You've made mountains that demonstrate Your grandeur. You protect us in the night hours and have placed glittering stars in the heavens, which You call by name. As I recount each blessing—I am awe-struck. How can my heart not respond with joy, with an overflowing sense of thanksgiving? Lord, may these return to You as my utmost expressions of adoration and praise. Amen.

God's wonders and blessings should "call forth joy" from within us daily. Try counting your blessings today and remember to find something in creation—because it's part of the Lord's love letter to your heart!

You have Redeemed my Soul!

"My lips will shout for joy, when I sing praises to you; my soul (inner being) also, which you have redeemed."
Psalm 71:23 ESV

Dear Lord, if I sent You a hand-written Christmas card—this verse would be the cry of my heart. I find myself so thankful this year—for Your care, blessings, Who You are to me, and how You're continually working in my life to transform me into Your image. Thanks for not giving up on me. Thanks for Your patient love and grace. Thank You for taking my hand through times of loss, pain, and things I cannot understand. Thank You for the unique opportunities to serve You this year, for how You've helped me grow in your knowledge, memorizing Scripture, and my trust. I sing praise to You. My soul, my inner being, is filled with joy.

I lift my hands and heart to exalt You. And I cannot thank You enough for calling me Your own. I need You, Jesus, and I bring the offering of my adoration as I bow before You, surrendered to do Your Will. Amen.

"Come, let us sing to the Lord! Let us shout joyfully to the Rock of our salvation." Psalm 95:1 NLT

....
....

If Jesus' blood has redeemed us—a song of joy should always grace our lips—because so great should be our gratitude that we cannot contain the gift that's been given to us!

A Meditation on What Child is This?

What Child is This? is a treasured carol that asks Who Jesus is. The lyrics answer the question with titles such as Christ the King, the Babe, and the Son of Mary. They encourage us to hasten to meet Him as each name gives Him identity and purpose.

In this section, you'll notice that I've taken some of Jesus' titles from Matthew 1-2, Luke 1, and John 1 to give God honor. Taking time to meditate upon these, as the Disciples did, is a way to draw near to the Lord. It's a way that we learn to love Him and discover His love for us personally. Because when we seek Jesus of the manger, we'll find that name fulfilled a mission—Immanuel—God with us, wants to dwell in our hearts.

When my siblings and I were younger, my grandmother sometimes "babysat" us when my parents enjoyed a weekend getaway. I remember her making a sugar candy—which I loved. During these times and our visits, she often shared with us about her "adopted" grandkids from other countries. She would "sponsor" little ones by providing a monthly $ amount. She did this for many years and would share their names and pictures with us.

She passed away in 1994. While in PA for her funeral, my husband and I offered to help my dad and aunt do a "first sort" of her things by cleaning her fridge and assisting with a few mundane chores. We helped to box like items etc. During that visit, I was given one of her books called 100 Names of God. It's one of my favorite things! I have read it repeatedly since her death—for encouragement, hope, comfort, and to praise the Lord. These Biblical titles like Alpha and Omega, Rock and Refuge, Prince of Peace and Rose of Sharon have given me a greater understanding of Who the Lord is and have helped me to deepen my faith in Him.

Let's look at a few of these types of names to answer the question—What Child Is This?

John 1:49 HCSB calls Him "'*Rabbi,' Nathanael replied, 'You are the Son of God! You are the King of Israel!'*"

John 6:35 NASB says: "*Jesus said to them, 'I am the bread of life; he who comes to Me will not hunger, and he who believes in Me will never thirst.'*"

John 8:12 NASB records: "*Then Jesus again spoke to them, saying, 'I am the Light of the world; he who follows Me will not walk in the darkness, but will have the Light of life.'*"

John 10:7 AMP testifies: "*So Jesus said again, I assure you and most solemnly say to you, I am the Door for the sheep [leading to life].'*"

John 10:14 AMP uses Jesus' own words to describe Himself: "*I am the Good Shepherd, and I know [without any doubt those who are] My own and My own know Me [and have a deep, personal relationship with Me].*"

In John 8:58 ISV, "*Jesus told them, 'Truly, I tell all of you emphatically, before there was an Abraham, I AM!'*"

Revelation 22:16 KJV records Jesus' words again, "*I Jesus have sent mine angel to testify unto you these things in the churches. I am the root and the offspring of David, and the bright and morning star.*"

The Babe, Jesus, is the same God that bears each of these names. Read each one and relate the title personally. Then thank the Lord for showing Himself to you in such profound ways.

You are the Messiah!

Messiah—
"When Jesus came to the region of Caesarea Philippi, he asked his disciples, 'Who do people say the Son of Man is?' They replied, 'Some say John the Baptist; others say Elijah; and still others, Jeremiah or one of the prophets.' 'But what about you?' he asked. 'Who do you say I am?' Simon Peter answered, 'You are the Messiah, the Son of the living God.'" Matthew 16:12-16 NIV

Dear Jesus, I love how You often ask questions. Here You put Your Disciples on the spot by quizzing them about the identity of the Son of Man (thus, Your perceived identity). They shared with You their various opinions and the rumors that had been spread throughout the region. But Peter displayed great courage and faith when he declared You to be the Messiah.

We must do likewise, believing this truth if You are to become the Lord of our lives. This moment of belief shows how he's seeking to follow everything You've been teaching them. And while Peter will waver at other moments, he will do great things for Your name and to acclaim Your renown. Help us to be as bold as he was in our stand for You, Lord, daily. Amen.

....
....

"Who do you say that Jesus is"? The answer is vital to your faith, testimony, and destiny.

Christ, the Anointed One!

Son Of Man—
"But Jesus kept silent and gave no answer at all. Again the high priest was questioning Him, and saying to Him, 'Are You the Christ (the Messiah, the Anointed), the Son of the Blessed One?' Jesus said, 'I am; and you will [all] see the Son of Man seated [with authority] at the right hand of Power (the Father), and coming with the clouds of heaven.'" Mark 14:61-62 AMP

Dear Jesus, there is much that we can learn about our communication from watching how You interacted with others, especially when You were being questioned or attacked by the Scribes and Pharisees. In this scene, a high priest asks You about Who You are. On the first pass of the question, You are silent. But when the question was repeated, You answered—clearly and articulately, "Yes, I am He." Lord, this example is precious to us as Your children. If such a question is put to us, may we answer with clarity—with faith and courage—never fearing to speak up or in any way be ashamed of You or Your Gospel message. Give us words to speak, O God, that draw others to Your heart and kingdom, we pray. Amen.

....

....

Jesus answered the question of Who He is—with clarity, authority, and the promise that He would come again. May we emulate His courage and rely on His strength to take a stand for Who You are in us, to us, and through us, O Lord.

This is my Beloved Son!

Son of God—
"While he was still speaking, a bright cloud
overshadowed them, and behold, a voice out of the
cloud said, 'This is My beloved Son, with whom I am
well-pleased; listen to Him!'" Matthew 17:5 NASB

Dear Jesus, I can only imagine the joy, surprise, and
wonder that filled the Disciples' hearts when they
witnessed a cloud descending and a voice proclaiming
You as God's beloved Son. What a holy day Your
baptism proved to be—as the Almighty's voice proudly
echoed that You are His child.

I wonder if any of Your followers dropped to their knees
in reverence, fear, or adoration? I wonder if their
countenances reflected a holy glow for hours to follow
this event. And I'm sure they listened a little more
closely to Your words and message in the coming days.
Lord, how we long to hear a similar refrain from You
when we stand before You face to face. Help us to listen,
obey, and seek to please You, Jesus, so that we're called
beloveds and told, "Well done, come into the supper of
the Lamb." Amen.

Do you have a desire to love and please God? To listen
to Him and obey Him? To seek Him daily? To call Him
Lord? These traits mark us as Christ-followers and
beloveds who are pleasing in the sight of our Savior,
Jesus Christ.

He is Mindful of Me!

God my Savior—
"My soul glorifies the Lord and my spirit rejoices in
God my Savior, for he has been mindful of the humble
state of his servant. From now on all generations will
call me blessed, for the Mighty One has done great
things for me—holy is his name." Luke 1:46-49 NIV

"The Lord is my strength and my song. He is my Savior.
This is my God, and I will praise him, my father's God,
and I will honor him." Exodus 15:2 GW

Dear Lord, this title "God my Savior" speaks softly and
loudly to my heart this Christmas season. Like Mary, my
soul exalts You. I'm always humbled to realize that
You're mindful of my slightest need, desire, joy, sorrow,
or longing. How I long to be Your servant, a useable
vessel. Daily I recount the ways that You're displaying
Your faithfulness to me. I feel blessed to read Your Word
and hear Your voice. You are my strength, the One I turn
to for counsel, comfort, wisdom, and guidance. You are
my God, my King, and my Savior. I bless Your holy
name and pray that my life gives You glory today and as
a legacy of faith. May every card I send, every gift I give,
and everything I share or do ... be filled with Your love
so that my love for You shines through. Amen.

If God is our Savior—we will want to know and love
Him personally—so that His Spirit is constantly filling
us so we have love flowing through us to be shared.

There is no God like You!

Lord, God of Israel—
"O LORD, God of Israel, there is no God like you in all
of heaven and earth. You keep your covenant and show
unfailing love to all who walk before you in
wholehearted devotion." 2 Chronicles 6:14 NLT

Dear Yahweh, in Genesis, You are Creator; in Revelation, You're called the Alpha and Omega. There is no god like You. There is no one above You. And there is no other way to Salvation (John 14:6, Acts 4:12), but through Your name. You are God to Your chosen people, the Jews, the nation of Israel. You are also God to the Gentiles through faith, grace, and Your work of redemption at the Cross.

Your promises are trustworthy and have endured for all time. Generation after generation has known Your loving kindness. And Your Word shall last forever. Your unfailing love surrounds us, reaches out to us, and embraces us as an invitation to be part of Your family. Lord, teach us to walk with You wholeheartedly and with an infectious joy that longs to give You praise. Amen.

<u>*Pause in the Word*</u>*: Please look up Mark 12:30, Joshua 22:5, Joshua 24:15, and Jeremiah 29:13. Think about a few things these verses have in common.*

God's Word, promises, and love—are steadfast, enduring, and everlasting—just like He is. That's why we know we can always trust Him, forever and devotedly.

The Heavens proclaim His Righteousness!

Ruler—
God the Supreme Ruler—"The Lord is king! Earth, be glad! Rejoice, you islands of the seas! Clouds and darkness surround him; he rules with righteousness and justice. ... The heavens proclaim his righteousness, and all the nations see his glory." Psalm 97:1-2 & 6 GNT

Father God, You are the ruler of the light, darkness, mountains, seas, and everything You've created from the beginning of time. You rule with might, power, truth, and justice. You rule the saints and angels who gather 'round Your throne. You lead my heart and life and are worthy of all praise. Everything falls under Your authority and divinity. All of mankind is subject to obey Your commands. Your majesty is evident in every page of Your holy Word. And there is no end to Your awe-inspiring miracles which Scripture tells us could not hold the volume of Your wondrous deeds. And while our praise will never be enough, we bring it. While our prayers will never be complete enough, we whisper them. While our thanksgiving will never express our gratitude, it's our offering.

Holy are You, Lord, we love You. Be the Ruler of our hearts and minds so that we surrender, obey, and glorify Your name upon the earth and heaven. Amen.

God is the ruler of it all—are you allowing Him to be the Ruler of your life? Home? Vocation? Family? Goals? Decisions? Dreams?

The Lord is my Shepherd!

Shepherd —
"The Lord is my Shepherd [to feed, to guide and to shield me], I shall not want. He lets me lie down in green pastures; He leads me beside the still and quiet waters." Psalm 23:1-2 AMP

Father God, there is no sweeter image than to envision You as my Shepherd. When I feel afraid, doubtful, or confused, I love to picture myself being held close in Your arms like a shepherd would a little lamb. This brings me comfort because it encourages me to rely on You to feed me, to care for my needs, to protect me, and to be my Guardian. Here, I'm safe. Here, I know I'm loved and feel at peace. I can rest in this tranquil setting simply by reading Your Word or baring my soul to Your throne — you still my anxious thoughts.

You take my hand and lead me beside a stream with a mountain view. I catch my breath, listen to the birdsong, and receive Your refreshment for my soul. Then I go out to share You in this way with others because many more sheep need to know (and respond) to Your voice. Then I'm ready to lie down and rest, knowing You're holding me close to Your heart. Amen.

....
....
....

If the Lord is our Shepherd, we will be like a little lamb — listening for His voice and following where He leads.

God's unfailing Love came through Jesus!

Unique One—
"From his abundance we have all received one gracious blessing after another. For the law was given through Moses, but God's unfailing love and faithfulness came through Jesus Christ. No one has ever seen God. But the unique One, who is himself God, is near to the Father's heart. He has revealed God to us." John 1:16-18 NLT

Dear Lord, when I think of Christmas, I naturally think of Your birth, the manger scene, Mary and Joseph, and the precious story from Luke that will be read in many churches and homes worldwide, including ours. I think of Your childhood and early years and how You were found to be teaching in the temple at the age of 12. I think of You at age 30, when You began Your ministry. And at 33, when You would give Your life—and love—for every man, woman, girl, and boy.

Your gift of grace was filled with abundant blessings, and from it flowed mercy, forgiveness, hope, joy, peace, and Your loving kindness.

You are the Unique One—the beloved Son of God—who is nearest to His heart. And yet, You have been revealed to us so that we too may share in Your kingdom. Thank You for loving us—and giving Your all for us—so that we can have everything, eternally. Amen.

The grace of God is our greatest present—for the past, present, and future!

GLORIA

In

Excelsis

Deo

A Meditation on Gloria in Excelsis Deo

The lyrics for this beloved carol are based on a Book of Common Prayer from 1662. The words focus on Jesus' deity, His holiness, and titles such as Heavenly King, Father Almighty, Jesu-Christ, and Lamb of God.

Gloria in Excelsis Deo means to give glory to God. Whether praise is represented by an angelic host—as is presented in the Luke 2 account of Jesus' birth, amid a Christmas Eve service or other worship settings, or our private offering of praise—it means that we offer adoration and thanksgiving to our Lord and Abba Daddy. It means that we intentionally set our minds on "things above," God's Word, or His attributes to see His faithfulness toward us.

I chose to focus these verses on the titles from Isaiah 9:6 because these have helped me to grow and know the Lord personally. These "names" have made my interactions with Jesus more meaningful. They have given me a rich and deeper understanding of His character and love for me. And I'm hoping they do the same for you.

God is Holy, Holy, Holy. He is Wonderful in all He's made, in His essence, wisdom, and power. He is our most excellent Counselor—giving us instruction, correction, and direction for every decision and step we take. He is our Almighty God, Who is omnipotent and omnipresent—available at all hours to each one of us. He is an Everlasting Father—Who has no beginning and no end. He is our Prince of Peace—calming every storm —bringing solace to body, mind, and spirit. He is the One true God—The Way, True, and Life—through Whom we are saved. And He is God Alone—the One Who is worthy of our praise —now and forevermore.

The God of creation is the same One to Whom every knee will bow, and every tongue confess that He is Lord (Philippians 2:9-11). The same Babe of the Manger is the same Messiah Who rules and reigns as the King of Kings. And the same Christ-child to Whom the angels sang "Glory to God in the highest" will be praised by the saints and angels 'round His throne for eternity.

"All honor and glory to God forever and ever! He is the eternal King, the unseen one who never dies; he alone is God. Amen." 1 Timothy 1:17 NLT

Dear Lord, how blessed it would have been to be among those who were gathered 'round the manger. But greater still, how magnificent to be gathered 'round Your throne, forever, to love, serve and honor You, and to sing Your praise. Gloria Excelsis Deo, indeed, to God alone be the Glory! Amen.

Below are some verses that reflect on the titles from Isaiah 9:6 but take you to other spots in the Bible. Take a few minutes to pause in each, then jot down your thoughts about how you can give God glory for each one.

Holy, Holy, Holy—Revelation 4:8
Wonderful—Isaiah 25:1
Counselor—Psalm 32:8
Almighty God—Psalm 24:10 & 80:19
Everlasting Father—Isaiah 40:28
Prince of Peace—2 Thessalonians 3:16
One True God—John 17:3
God Alone—Romans 16:25-27

....
....

Holy, is the Lord of Hosts!

Holy, Holy, Holy—
"Above Him seraphim (heavenly beings) stood; each one had six wings: with two wings he covered his face, with two wings he covered his feet, and with two wings he flew. And one called out to another, saying, 'Holy, Holy, Holy is the Lord of hosts; The whole earth is filled with His glory.'" Isaiah 6:2-3 AMP

Father God, the sound of all the heavenly beings joined with one chorus of praise fills my mind and heart with joy. These majestic seraphim, described as having six wings, inspire awe. With wings representing glory, humility, and surrender, they illustrate giving You our worship and adoration alone. Holy, Holy, Holy are You, Abba Daddy. Earth and heaven are filled with Your wonders, miracles, and everlasting love. Your sovereignty over all of time and space, over light, over every living and breathing thing—takes my breath away. How could we do anything but lift our voices and hands—to proclaim as Master and Adonai—and bow right along with the angels—to glorify Your name? Amen.

(See Philippians 2:9-11—see especially the AMP translation). We will cry out "hosannas" and laud Him as our Savior and dearest Companion.

We declare Jesus to be holy—because He is worthy of our complete devotion due to His righteousness, He is divine in nature, part of the Godhead (deity), and sacred (or set apart) as our sinless sacrifice Who rose from the dead to give us eternal life.

You have done Wonderful Things!

Wonderful—
"O Lord, You are my God. I will exalt You, I will praise Your name, for You have done wonderful things; Your counsels of old are faithfulness and truth." Isaiah 25:1 NKJV

Jehovah, You are wonderful in all Your ways—loving, kind, gracious, forgiving, and merciful. You are just, trustworthy, and omnipotent. Your holiness knows no bounds. Your authority cannot be challenged. Your wisdom is unmatched. Your faithfulness reaches the heights of heaven. And we can never give You enough glory, honor, or praise for Who You are. Yet, You invite us to come to You. You draw us near to worship—to bring our hearts of gratitude and adoration near. You encourage us to bring every need before Your throne. You desire an intimate relationship with us so that we grow in our knowledge of You and our love for You. And You alone, O Lord, hold the keys to death, life, and our eternal security. My hope is in You and Your Salvation, Jesus, not because of anything I've done but because of Your grace and love toward me (and all mankind). I trust You, Lord. You are a good, good Father. I'm an ever-grateful child. Amen.

Do you know Jesus as Your Wonderful ... Comforter, Protector, Refuge, and Healer? Think about your greatest need ... then tell Jesus that He's Your wonderful _____. This daily exercise will show You God's presence and a pattern of His faithfulness in your life.

I am confident He will care for my Own!

Counselor—
"The Spirit of truth will come and guide you in all truth. He will not speak His own words to you; He will speak what He hears, revealing the things to come and bringing glory to Me. The Spirit has unlimited access to Me, to all I possess and know, just as everything the Father has is Mine. That is why I am confident He will care for My own and reveal the path to you." John 16:13
VOICE

Dear Lord, I am so thankful for the many roles of Your Holy Spirit in my life. Thank You for the truths that You speak into my heart when I read and meditate upon Your Word. Teach me, Jesus, to walk in Your ways. Guide my decisions as I take delight in Your presence. Reveal to me how to love You and others as You would desire—so that I serve You with joy and gladness.

Father God, it overwhelms me to know that I have unlimited access to Your throne room—Your presence at all hours of the day and night. Jesus, show me daily how to reflect Your attributes to those around me and praise You wholeheartedly. Amen.

....
....
....

We can have confidence in Christ as our Counselor—
because when we receive Jesus as our Lord and Savior,
His Spirit indwells us to become our Advisor,
Intercessor, Defender, and Prince of Peace.

I AM the Alpha and Omega!

Almighty God—
"'I am the Alpha and the Omega—the beginning and the end,' says the Lord God. 'I am the one who is, who always was, and who is still to come—the Almighty One.'" Revelation 1:8 NLT

Heavenly Father, as I think about these precious names of Yours from Isaiah 9:6, this one—"Almighty God" thrills my heart. I loved the reminder from Revelation 1:8 that You are the Beginning and End—of creation, of our every breath, of every circumstance, of the earth and heaven, and of eternity. Your power is amazing to meditate upon.

Your strength and might are endless. And Your love is all-encompassing. You existed before time began. You are at work in the visible and invisible. And You will forever reign in our hearts and upon Your throne. For Your omnipresence, we exalt You. Amen.

"Then I heard again what sounded like the shout of a vast crowd or the roar of mighty ocean waves or the crash of loud thunder: 'Praise the Lord! For the Lord our God, the Almighty, reigns.'" Revelation 1:8 NLT

....
....
....

Our Lord is an Almighty God—Who loves and saves us, Who was, is, and forever reigns over the earth, heaven, and eternity. His power can take care of your every need!

The Lord is the Everlasting God!

Everlasting Father—
"Do you not know? Have you not heard? The LORD is the everlasting God, the Creator of the ends of the earth. He will not grow tired or weary, and his understanding no one can fathom." Isaiah 40:28 NIV

Dear Jesus, I love the places in Scripture that ask us questions. Isaiah is making a point about Your character by engaging our minds and hearts and driving us deeper into our understanding of Who You are. And following these questions comes the answer. You are everlasting. You are the Creator in terms of the Genesis account of the world, but also of every person and every heart's desire to know You. You do not tire. You do not grow weary of our questions, providing our answers, meeting our needs, interacting with us, or hearing our praise.

Thank You for welcoming us, Lord, like children, but helping us to mature in our faith so that we know more of Your ways year by year. You are fathomless, and our pursuit in Your Word and in Your company shall not cease. Amen.

How have you heard or known God to be your Everlasting Father?

....
....

We must spend time with the Lord to know Him and hear Him speak into our lives. It's then that we learn how awesome, powerful, holy, and loving He is to each of us.

The Lord of Compassion

Prince of Peace—
"'Though the mountains be shaken and the hills be removed, yet my unfailing love for you will not be shaken nor my covenant of peace be removed,' says the Lord, who has compassion on you." Isaiah 54:10 NIV

Dear Jesus, knowing You as Prince of Peace has been a blessing to my life. Learning about being still in Your presence (Psalm 46:10) or how You calmed the waves during a storm with Your Disciples (Mark 4:35-41) continually teaches me to rely upon You for our smallest or greatest needs. And here in Isaiah 54:10, You provide another excellent example and promise of Your loving nature toward us. Though mountains be shaken (literally or figuratively) ... though hills be removed (during times of loss, disappointment, or uncertainty), Your peace will meet us, comfort us, and assure us of Your nearness. Father, remind me of these promises often. Help me in moments of fear or doubt to step out in faith, take Your hand in trust, and walk on the waves to dwell in Your peace. I believe You're with me, living in me, and always faithful to Your word. Amen.

Jesus is called the Prince of Peace because He's known for calming any wave, bringing solace to any circumstance, and teaching us that He has compassion for us which will never be removed. So let us stand firm in our love for Him and rest in these promises. And may the peace that comes with Christmas abide in your heart all year through.

One Lord, One God, and Father of All.

Give the One True God Honor—
"Yet for us, there is but one God, the Father, who is the
source of all things, and we exist for Him; and one Lord,
Jesus Christ, by whom are all things [that have been
created], and we [believers exist and have life and have
been redeemed] through Him." 1 Corinthians 8:6 AMP

"There is one Lord, one faith, one baptism, one God and
Father of all, who is over all, in all, and living through
all." Ephesians 4:5-6 NLT

Dear Heavenly Father, I give You my praise and
adoration because You are sovereign, holy, majestic, and
deserving of every honor. There is One God (as clearly
stated in these verses). There is One faith through which
we are saved. There is One baptism that anoints us with
the power of the Holy Spirit. And there is One Savior
who lives in the heart of every Christ-follower who calls
Him Lord. You redeemed us through Your blood and
gave us right standing—or dressed us in righteousness—
through Your grace and forgiveness. We exist to love You
as You have loved us. And to sing of Your glorious
goodness is a privilege, Jesus.

It engages my soul with joy and a sense of thanksgiving.
And it helps me focus on Who You are—instead of my
earthly problems. Thank You, Lord, for being worthy of
all praise. Amen.

When we sing of Lord's glory, we are surrendering to
His power and authority. We are trusting Him as the
One true God, the Author and Perfecter of our faith.

You alone are God!

Soli Deo Gloria — God Alone —
"No pagan god is like you, O Lord. None can do what you do! All the nations you made will come and bow before you, Lord; they will praise your holy name. For you are great and perform wonderful deeds. You alone are God. Teach me your ways, O Lord, that I may live according to your truth! Grant me purity of heart so that I may honor you. With all my heart, I will praise you, O Lord my God. ..." Psalm 86:8-12 NLT

Dear Lord, in Exodus 20:3, You instructed us to have no other gods before You. No one can compare with Your glory, splendor, or beauty. You have shown Yourself to us through the wonders of creation. You have made Yourself visible through Your miracles and the healing power of Your Holy Word. You have given us the gifts of hymns, choruses, and the Psalms to worship and bring You our adoration. You're attentive to our cries and our pleas. And You are present to celebrate our triumphs, to forgive us, and to help us begin again when we fail. You change us, restore us, and redeem us. So, Jesus, we come with praise, tithes, offerings, with hearts that overflow with gratitude to love and serve You. We cherish our relationship with You and wish to sit at Your feet and learn from Your instructions until we see You face to face. Amen.

Soli Deo Gloria — to God, alone be the glory. There is none other Who is worthy of our praise. There is no other to Whom — all — will give an account. And there is no other way to Salvation — except through knowing Him as — Master, Abba Daddy, and Friend. May God be praised!

O
COME
All
Ye
FAITHFUL
ooo

A Meditation on
O Come All Ye Faithful

O Come All Ye Faithful is a cherished carol, isn't it? I love how it invites us to pause for a few moments in the village of Bethlehem and also at the throne of God to give Him honor. I treasure how it encourages us to "behold Him" and inspires us to be counted among those faithfully following His Word's decrees and ways.

I've always valued the places in Scripture where God asks His Disciples about their lack of faith. We can learn a great deal from their doubts, fears, and times of wavering—mainly because we can identify with them, right? We have mountain-top experiences and times when we feel so close to the Lord, and then "wham," something happens, and we ask, "Where are You, Lord?" We share the same insecurities and have the same questions that they did. And we can walk with the Lord, just as they did, and yet miss what He's trying to teach us.

Let's look at two example passages and see what we can glean about faith and about raising our level of trust in the One Who is worthy of our following and devotion.

"And when they had come to the multitude, a man came to Him, kneeling down to Him and saying, 'Lord, have mercy on my son, for he is an epileptic and suffers severely; for he often falls into the fire and often into the water. So I brought him to Your disciples, but they could not cure him.' Then Jesus answered and said, 'O faithless and perverse generation, how long shall I be with you? How long shall I bear with you? Bring him here to Me.' And Jesus rebuked the demon, and it came out of him; and the child was cured from that very hour. ...

...Then the disciples came to Jesus privately and said, 'Why could we not cast it out?' So Jesus said to them, 'Because of your unbelief; for assuredly, I say to you, if you have faith as a mustard seed, you will say to this mountain, 'Move from here to there,' and it will move; and nothing will be impossible for you. However, this kind does not go out except by prayer and fasting.'" Matthew 17:14-21 NKJV

"Then, turning to his disciples, Jesus said, 'That is why I tell you not to worry about everyday life—whether you have enough food to eat or enough clothes to wear. For life is more than food, and your body more than clothing. Look at the ravens. They don't plant or harvest or store food in barns, for God feeds them. And you are far more valuable to him than any birds! Can all your worries add a single moment to your life? And if worry can't accomplish a little thing like that, what's the use of worrying over bigger things? Look at the lilies and how they grow. They don't work or make their clothing, yet Solomon in all his glory was not dressed as beautifully as they are. And if God cares so wonderfully for flowers that are here today and thrown into the fire tomorrow, he will certainly care for you. Why do you have so little faith? ... Seek the Kingdom of God above all else, and he will give you everything you need. So don't be afraid, little flock. For it gives your Father great happiness to give you the Kingdom.'" Luke 12:22-32 NLT (excerpts).

In the first illustration from Matthew 17, the Disciples ask why they could not do what Jesus did—by healing this lad. Jesus' answer includes faith, prayer, and fasting. In other words—He wants them to have a deeper trust and relationship with the Father than they are currently experiencing. To date, they have witnessed Jesus doing miracles. They are growing. And they are learning to know Him, but He wants to take them beyond this point—into a Spirit-led action—that goes beyond knowing God can do something to empowering them to do it in His stead.

In the second instance from Luke—Jesus asks them why they are still exhibiting so little faith. He uses creation to display His ability to clothe and provide for the birds and the flowers as a means of asking why they, and we, sometimes question His protection and faithfulness. I love how Jesus calls us "little flock." This implies a personal, caring, and intimate interaction with Him as our Shepherd. It reminds us that He is always tending to our needs and wants us to live in a state of dependence upon Him with a lack of fear or doubt in His ability to provide what we need. Here, we are encouraged to seek His kingdom. A lack of faith on our part—keeps us from experiencing all that God intends for us. It keeps us from knowing and desiring Him. And it stands in our way of full obedience. So, let's strive to plant mustard seeds of faith—and watch the Lord turn them into trees and fields—as we surrender every area of our lives and hearts to His care.

Has the Spirit led you to any area that you're not trusting to Jesus' care? If so, surrender a prayer, now. What steps can you take to deepen your faith and trust in the Lord?

Here are a few other places worth beholding: Hebrews 11:1 & 6, 2 Corinthians 5:7, Deuteronomy 7:9, Luke 7:50, John 20:29.

....
....
....
....
....
....
....
....
....

Great is His Faithfulness!

"Great is his faithfulness; his mercies begin afresh each morning. I say to myself, 'The Lord is my inheritance; therefore, I will hope in him!'" Lamentations 3:23-24 NLT

Dear Jesus, there's nothing like a fresh coat of snow in Winter to give the brown earth a fresh, new appearance. It's like a coating of grace has dropped from heaven to remind us of Your forgiveness, like wool. Great is Your faithfulness! Your mercy arrives like dawn to make the landscape sparkle and shine. My heart is filled with hope and joy. I celebrate this season by finding unique beauty in it—like ice formations or watching the waves freeze in place or by finding delight in kids ice skating or how the sun sets upon a lake to form rainbows. Thank You, Lord, for Your mercies that surround me daily and for giving me the gift of Salvation—my inheritance in Your presence—eternally. You are my hiding place from the cold winds, the One I run to and seek for my every need. Amen.

Pause in the Word: Please look up 1 Thessalonians 5:24, 2 Thessalonians 3:3-5, and Psalm 36:5. Jot down your insights about God's faithfulness.

....
....
....

No matter the weather, no matter the season, God's faithfulness is beyond compare. Daily, it is His gift to us—the inheritance and hope—of our Salvation.

The Lord is Faithful

"Therefore know [without any doubt] and understand that the Lord your God, He is God, the faithful God, who is keeping His covenant and His [steadfast] lovingkindness to a thousand generations with those who love Him and keep His commandments." Deuteronomy 7:9 AMP

Father God, thank You for Your faithful love and attention. Thank You for the covenants You've made with humanity throughout the Bible. These promises gave hope to Your chosen people, and they continue to encourage the hearts of Your children today. Your Word is everlasting. And Your truths are a heritage that we have to share with our family, friends, and loved ones.

They are the legacy of our faith and a testimony of trusting our lives to Your care. Grant us wisdom, Jesus, to know and discern Your Spirit's leading. And helps us obey Your Will — by being attentive to Your voice. Amen.

"Not to us, O Lord, not to us, but to your name give glory, for the sake of your steadfast love and your faithfulness!" Psalm 115:1 ESV

....
....

Do not doubt the faithfulness of God. His lovingkindness is steadfast, just like His Word. It reaches back through time and will advance through every generation until His return.

I will exalt You, O Lord!

"O Lord, You are my God. I will exalt You, I will praise Your name, For You have done wonderful things; Your counsels of old are faithfulness and truth." Isaiah 25:1 NKJV

Dear Heavenly Father, You are my God, Rock, and Refuge. I come before You singing praises, carols, and hymns in this holiday season to exalt Your holy name. I love joining my voice with others in a harmonious sound to celebrate Your precious Son's birth. These words that often come directly from Scripture have become a welcome tradition that grounds our lives. They help us remember times when we were younger and when we went caroling from house to house. They take us back to the manger scene and help us picture You as a Babe. And they help us worship You as our Master and King of Kings.

Thank You for the gift of these cherished verses and the writers who brought them to life. For like Your Holy Word, they are precious to us and speak truth into our hearts in the form of music that shall endure for all time. Amen.

....
....

Christmas carols can be heard in churches, in shops, and echoing on the streets. They are often based on God's Word and keep His truths near to our hearts through their faithful testimony of music, which brings us joy.

Take Refuge!

"With his feathers he will cover you, and under his wings you can take refuge. His faithfulness will be a shield and a buckler." Psalm 91:4 LEB

Dear Lord, I love to conjure this image in my mind of You covering me — as a bird would its young by opening its feathers — in a gesture of protection, love, and care. We had a nest of robins illustrate this so perfectly one Spring. The parent did precisely this. It stretched its wings outward over all of its chicks until they were invisible to the naked eye. That's what You do for us, Jesus.

You're our refuge, our shield, our guardian. I had to do a little research on the term "buckler" for a previous study. Did you know that it is slightly smaller than a shield yet a mighty weapon in times of war? That's our Savior. And again, I cherish these vivid ways that He portrays Himself that are so easily understood. Thank You, Father, for being ever-present and loving us with everlasting, never-ending faithfulness. Amen.

"Blessed be the Lord who has given rest to his people Israel, according to all that he promised. Not one word has failed of all his good promise, which he spoke by Moses his servant." I Kings 8:56 ESV

If you ever need to feel the protection and guardianship of the Lord, picture yourself as a baby chick and Him lovingly spreading His feathers over you to hide you with His love.

Trust in the Lord with all Your Heart!

"Let not steadfast love and faithfulness forsake you; bind them around your neck; write them on the tablet of your heart. So you will find favor and good success in the sight of God and man. Trust in the Lord with all your heart, and do not lean on your own understanding. In all your ways acknowledge him, and he will make straight your paths." Proverbs 3:3-6 ESV

Dear Jesus, this is one of my favorite life passages from Your Holy Word. These words bring comfort, guidance, and wisdom during difficult circumstances. They have challenged, instructed, and encouraged me. And they have brought me nearer to Your presence to seek Your Will. Lord, I treasure Your love and faithfulness. I'm writing more and more of Your Word upon my heart every day. I'm memorizing it and applying it to every situation. I'm learning to trust You with greater depth. And I'm always quick to acknowledge my sin and need for You daily.

Make straight my paths, Father, for I want my steps to emulate Yours. Grant me Your favor and a good reputation as I seek to be an ambassador of Your truths and commands. Amen.

Trusting God means that we seek Him for everything. Then we actively watch for His presence and hand to guide and direct us. Over time, we'll see a trail of His faithfulness, which brings us back to trusting Him more and more.

We Rejoice in hope of the Glory of God!

"Therefore, since we have been justified by faith, we have peace with God through our Lord Jesus Christ. Through him we have also obtained access by faith into this grace in which we stand, and we rejoice in hope of the glory of God." Romans 5:1-2 ESV

Dear Lord, as I was researching verses for the "O Come All Ye Faithful" section, this one leaped out at me because it conveys the message of Your goodness to those who have surrendered our hearts to You. We've been justified through faith and Your generous gift of grace. You've clothed us with peace. You've given us hope—of eternity in Your presence—and of walking with You each day. We commune with You by reading Your Word, praying, and listening for Your voice. We are invited to bring everything before Your throne. And we praise You for the ordinary and extraordinary ways You provide for our needs.

Your faithfulness, O God, inclines my heart to be faithful and disciplined in the pursuit of knowing You and growing and maturing in You. Teach us day by day, Jesus, that You are accessible 24/7 and help us not to withhold anything from Your domain. Amen.

....
....

Being justified by Jesus means that our faith is made stronger, purer, and refined daily so that we rejoice in the hope we've found! It means drawing near to God so that He can use us to draw others into His kingdom.

Lord, the Honor belongs to You!

"Lord, you should receive the honor, not us. The honor belongs to you because of your faithful love and loyalty." Psalm 115:1 ERV

Dear Lord, Thank You for Your faithful care and attention, and for meeting our needs. I'm reminded of my high school glee club days. We had a Christmas program each year, and we would enter the auditorium in a single file, holding a candle while singing "O Come All Ye Faithful." The sound was so beautiful, echoing around the people who attended as we made our way to the stage. The light enveloped the room as if to embrace the space. I always felt like You were being invited into our procession. It seemed like a holy beginning to our holiday presentation as we sang these beloved carols. I know in my heart I desired to give You honor. I brought You my best through our practices and our concerts. And as we looked out over the crowd, I always loved to see those who appeared to worship with us. Unto You, Lord, we bring our love and adoration. We lift our voices, hands, and hearts to declare You our precious King. Amen.

What Christmas tradition do you or your family practice that solely focuses on honoring Jesus? If you don't have one—such as going to a candlelight service, reading Luke 2 as a family, or buying Jesus an ornament each year—perhaps you'll adopt one of these. Others might include giving a Christmas tithe (as the Wisemen brought gold, frankincense, and myrrh) or gathering your loved ones and expressing gratitude for God's graciousness during this year.

Well done, good and faithful Servant!

"His master said to him, 'Well done, good and faithful servant. You have been faithful and trustworthy over a little, I will put you in charge of many things; share in the joy of your master.'" Matthew 25:21 AMP

Father God, it's the prayer of every heart to hear these words when we stand before You. How cherished they are ... to receive as the evaluation of our lives, our time on earth. That's our desire, Lord. Teach us to be faithful and trustworthy—in our jobs, relationships, and with the things that You give us to be stewards of.

Help us acknowledge that all we have comes from Your gracious hand. And Jesus, let us have hearts that love and serve You—working unto You—no matter how grand or menial our daily tasks so that we stand out as Your representative. Let the joy that we have because of You—shine forth like the sun—on earth and in Your kingdom to come. Amen.

....
....
....

When you get to the close of each day ... this is a good question: Would Jesus say to me? "Well done, good and faithful servant?" If the answer is yes, at the end of each one ... keep doing what you're doing—loving, serving, giving, and emulating His ways. If not ... ask Him how to make tomorrow closer to His image. This is a prayer He will answer because it displays a seeking attitude.

WHITE
Christmas

A Meditation on White Christmas

What do you think of when you hear the phrase "White Christmas?" Does it evoke childhood memories like snowball fights, sled riding, and caroling in your neighborhood? How about having a day or two off from school? Do they bring to mind special gatherings with your family and friends? How about traditions like cutting a fresh evergreen? Or having popcorn and hot cocoa around the fireplace? I'm sure you have memories from the past coming to mind. This carol even inspired a famous movie/musical that has endured through the years to become a beloved tradition in its own right.

Doug and I love a white Christmas and snow in general. We have, from the time that we were kids, and except for shoveling, we still do. We enjoy watching the crystalline, glittering flakes fall. We like to see how snow drifts on country roads and along fences. We love how it varies from a fine texture to down-like feathers and covers winter's barrenness. In fact, that's how I began to see it as an analogy for God's grace.

This section will highlight snow—by spotlighting it in creation. We'll also look at how God's Word uses it as an analogy for covering our sins through His forgiveness. So, let's read a passage from Isaiah 55 that gives us both perspectives to see how this favorite carol can inspire us to appreciate this wonder that falls from heaven to grace earth with such beauty.

Isaiah 55:1, 3, 6-13 NLT "Is anyone thirsty? Come and drink. ... Come to me with your ears wide open. Listen, and you will find life. I will make an everlasting covenant with you. I will give you all the unfailing love I promised to David. ... Seek the Lord while you can find him. Call on him now while he is near. Let the wicked change their ways, and banish the very thought of doing wrong. Let them turn to the Lord that he may have mercy on them. Yes, turn to our God, for he will forgive generously. ...

... 'My thoughts are nothing like your thoughts,' says the Lord. 'And my ways are far beyond anything you could imagine. For just as the heavens are higher than the earth, so my ways are higher than your ways and my thoughts higher than your thoughts.' The rain and snow come down from the heavens and stay on the ground to water the earth. They cause the grain to grow, producing seed for the farmer and bread for the hungry. It is the same with my word. I send it out, and it always produces fruit. It will accomplish all I want it to, and it will prosper everywhere I send it. You will live in joy and peace. The mountains and hills will burst into song, and the trees of the field will clap their hands! Where once there were thorns, cypress trees will grow. Where nettles grew, myrtles will sprout up. These events will bring great honor to the Lord's name; they will be an everlasting sign of his power and love."

This passage begins with a question: Is anyone thirsty? Then notice that we are given several directives to answer: 1) Come to Me. 2) Listen. 3) Seek the Lord. 4) Call on Him. 5) Make a change. 6) Turn to the Lord.

Spend a few minutes contemplating these directives. Is Jesus speaking in any area? Jot down what you hear from His Spirit. Is there any action the Lord is asking you to take or correction He's asking you to make?

....

Notice the list of items of creation: rain, snow, seed, fruit, mountains, hills, trees. How do the things that He's fashioned— remind you of blessings (or faithfulness) from His hand?

....

Notice what God's Word produces: growth, joy, and peace. It goes where He sends it. It brings honor to His name. It brings life and instills praise. Meditate on these actions, and record how they can take root in your heart.

....

God Speaks and it Snows!

"For He says to the snow, fall on the earth; likewise He speaks to the showers and to the downpour of His mighty rains." Job 37:6 AMPC

Dear Lord, though You allowed Job's faith to be tested, I love how He continually pointed to Your power and sovereignty. He knew that You are—in all, above all, and working through all that You've made. This helped him trust You during the greatest trial of his life. It encourages us to do the same.

Job 37:6 tells us that You "say to the snow—fall." You give a directive, and even the climate obeys You. You speak to the rain, and it showers the earth to bring about a harvest of crops and flowers and to sustain life. These things that You've formed do as You command them.

Jesus, may I obey Your Word and voice likewise. May I be sensitive to Your Spirit's promptings and seek to believe in You—even during the most challenging moments—simply because You are my Lord and my God. Amen.

....
....
....

The Lord spoke in Genesis, and creation answered. It's the same here in Job. This illustration of God's power empowered Job to trust the Lord. It should do the same in us too!

Snow like Wool

"God spread snow like it was wool; God scatters frost like it was ashes; God throws his hail down like crumbs —who can endure God's freezing cold? Then God issues his word and melts it all away! God makes his winds blow; the water flows again." Psalm 147:16-18 CEB

Dear Jesus, a fresh coat of feathery down has begun to fall outside the window. I see it reflected in the streetlamp and watch the flakes dance and swirl in the wind. You're creating a wintery wonderland, a beautiful scene covering all that is drab and brown. I love to watch You paint the landscape with Your grace and purity.

It reminds me of a bride dressing for her wedding day. The snow that lands on the tree limbs appears as filmy as her veil. Her gown is the covering that forms and drifts over every texture and tapestry of the earth. Her shoes are like patterned leather where ice forms. And the glittering wonderment—appears as her jeweled accents. Then just like this precious ceremony ... too soon, the day is over, the storm passes, and the scene is gone. But still, we see Your beauty, splendor, and majesty. And we wait anxiously for the next day when You spread snow like wool, frost like ashes ... and remind us again of Your grace. Amen.

....
....

Snow is a magical gift of Winter, God's creations, and a symbol of His purity and grace.

God's Word, Like Snow, Will Yield Seed

"As the rain and snow come down from heaven, and do not return to it without watering the earth and making it bud and flourish so that it yields seed for the sower and bread for the eater, so is my word that goes out from my mouth; it will not return to me empty, but will accomplish what I desire and achieve the purpose for which I sent it." Isaiah 55:10-11 NIV

Dear Lord, I love how rain and snow nourish the earth. Each arrives and falls in its perfect season to prepare or bring new life. These nutrients descend from heaven, and Your hand causes the seed to grow and plants, flowers, and crops to flourish. So it is with your Word. Wherever it's planted, it yields a harvest. Wherever it is shared, it will take root. Wherever the Gospel is spread, it is fertilized to cause an increase. You promise that it will not return to You empty. And though You also share a parable of seeds being sown on various kinds of soil — Luke 8:4-15 — we must trust that You will use our efforts for the good of others and Your glory. Father, let Your Word be planted in my heart each day and let me be a planter of Your truth to those around me. Amen.

....

God promises to take His Word — and use it for His purposes. This takes the pressure off us because we only have to plant the seeds and trust Him for the harvest. We are not responsible for the "yield" only for what has been entrusted to us. Are you sowing (memorizing, applying, and sharing) the pure and holy Word of God?

Our Sins can be White like Snow

"Come now, let us reason together, says the LORD: though your sins are like scarlet, they shall be as white as snow; though they are red like crimson, they shall become like wool." Isaiah 1:18 ESV

Dear Jesus, I love this child-like imagery of snow—pure white snow—as a covering and a sign of Your grace and forgiveness. In Psalm 103:11-12 we're told that You remove our transgressions as far as the east is from the west. Often, the snow paints the landscape of a field like this—as far as the eye can see—and I'm reminded of this precious promise from Your Word. Though our wrongs are like the darkest red stain, You make them as white as a lamb's wool.

These simple word pictures touch our hearts and help us see You in a fresh light. They help us imagine every day as a clean slate—a new beginning. And You're inviting us into conversation, prayer, and fellowship—as we confess our wrongdoing—and exchange our sorrowful habit or behavior for the right relationship that You restore. Amen.

<u>*Pause in the Word*</u>*: Please look up Romans 3:23-24, Romans 6:23, and Titus 3:5. How do these verses help you appreciate Jesus' mercy and forgiveness?*

Come into the presence of Jesus; acknowledge every imperfection to the sinless Son of God, then let Him wash You white as snow!

Wash me with Hyssop

"Purify me from sin with hyssop, and I will be clean. Wash me, and I will be whiter than snow." Psalm 51:7 GW

Dear Lord, as I come to meet with You, I love how You challenge me to learn and grow. For instance, the curiosity you instilled in me made me want to examine what hyssop looks or smells like. And when I seek— You answer. If you're wondering too ... Hyssop is an herbaceous plant described as a cross between mint, anise, and oregano. It is sometimes used for tea and is considered to have healing properties. Notice the beloved irony of our God? Purify me—from my sin, Psalm 51:7 says, with hyssop—with the healing balm of His grace which washes us clean, and restores us into right relationship with His Spirit. Like snow—white, holy, pure.

What an image this portrays to our hearts, O God. How we long for this type of medicine from You, our Jehovah Rapha! We come to You with our every fault and frailty, knowing You are sinless and always ready to take us in Your arms. Amen.

Christmas time yields many emotions. If all of your memories and life experiences are not perfect, let Jesus bring healing like hyssop to your heart, mind, and soul. In fact, if there's snow on the ground where you live— be like a kid and make a snow angel—to get covered in the down of His grace. Laugh. And be embraced by Your Abba Daddy and Great Physician!

Praise the Lord from Heaven!

"Praise the Lord from heaven! Praise God on the heights! Praise God, all of you who are his messengers! ... Sun and moon, praise God! All of you bright stars, praise God! You highest heaven, praise God! Do the same, you waters that are above the sky! Let all of these praise the Lord's name. ... Do the same ... hail, snow and smoke, stormy wind that does what God says! Do the same, you mountains, every single hill, fruit trees, and every single cedar! Do the same, you animals—wild or tame—you creatures that creep along and you birds that fly! (snow, cold, etc) ... Let all of these praise the Lord's name because only God's name is high over all." Psalm 148 excerpts. CEB

Dear Jesus, I thank You that it's easy for my heart to praise You. I cherish seeing Your presence in creation, as Romans 1:20 articulates, as Your way of conveying Your love to all mankind. I love watching You paint a sunrise or sunset and thinking of You as an Artist. I marvel at snow-capped mountains in the Winter, which You drape with beautiful wildflowers in the Summer. I'm mesmerized by the sea's waves—by their power and Your majesty. I like to behold the myriad types of animals You've made, from great to small. In every season and changing landscape, I observe Your grandeur and holiness. I lift my hands and bow my knees because I'm so grateful for all You've made and for Who You are. Amen.

Let everyone that has breath "Praise the Lord."

He Refreshes his Master like Snow

"Like the cold of snow [brought from the mountains] in the time of harvest, so is a faithful messenger to those who send him; for he refreshes the life of his masters." Proverbs 25:13 AMP

Dear Jesus, You know how much our cat, Tilly, loves snow. She gets excited as the first flakes begin to fall. She is even more delighted when a bowl of this refreshing, beautiful, glistening substance is delivered. She dips her paws in immediately. Her joy is palpable. Without words, she conveys a message to us that she is grateful for this treat. This is much like the image You're creating with these words to us.

Snow—refreshes—the landscape from its barrenness. It refreshes us when we are hiking in the woods. So is a faithful servant or message to His master. So are we to You when we obey, read Your Word, and follow Your Will for our lives. And practicing these daily habits also refreshes the lives of others since they instill in us character, perseverance, and greater steps of faith. Lord, may Your Spirit pour love, joy, gentleness, goodness, faith, meekness, and temperance ... into our souls daily so we bring peace to every space that we enter. Amen.

....
....

In every season, we are a messenger of something. Through the Holy Spirit—we can bring a sense of refreshment to God's heart and the hearts of others. Lord, may it be so!

His Hair is like Snow.

"His head and hair were white like wool, as white as snow, and His eyes like a flame of fire; His feet were like fine brass, as if refined in a furnace, and His voice as the sound of many waters; He had in His right hand seven stars, out of His mouth went a sharp two-edged sword, and His countenance was like the sun shining in its strength." Rev. 1:14-16 NKJV

Almighty God, this picture of You from Revelation is awe-inspiring. The Apostle John was given a glimpse of Your holiness, Your radiance—and this is the description he transcribes to us. You're described as having hair that's as pure as snow. Your eyes are depicted—as discerning like flames. Your feet are as prized, purified metal that appears glorified. Your voice thunders like the sea. You hold glorious stars in Your hands, and Your mouth will share Your Holy Word with clarity and truth. Your face will illumine the heavens where there is no need for the sun or moon because You are the Light. And every knee will bow, and every tongue will confess that You are God (Philippians 2:9-11). Hallowed be Your name, O Lord, to You alone is the glory, power, and honor forever. You are the King of Kings and Savior of my life. And it will be my pleasure to give You my adoration, eternally. Amen.

Descriptions of God's holiness are meant to bring us into His holy presence, to teach us to fear and revere Him, and above all, to give us an inspired view of our great Savior's power, authority, sovereignty, and all-encompassing love.

O

Holy

NIGHT

▪ ▪ ▪

A Meditation on O Holy Night

Each morning and evening, I spend time memorizing Scripture. As I have shared in several "dedications," I have thyroid disease. While not everyone's experience is the same—in me—this means sometimes having trouble getting the right words when I am writing or speaking, having a mild form of dyslexia, or having difficulty retaining these precious truths as I try to learn them. This has been further compounded by a concussion that is taking a long time to heal.

I find that the verses that I learned as a child—have been retained. But the new ones that I am inputting—need constant repetition. Here's a tip: if you have children or grandchildren or are in a position to influence young ones—encourage them to memorize God's Word and promises! I can't stress it enough. And a fun fact? In Jesus' time—Jewish boys were taught to do this from age 5.

Doug and I were blessed to have something called "Released Time,"—a traveling Bible bus that visited our schools. We were taught from God's Word and memorized Scripture as part of this weekly event. In fact, it was connected to a local camp—called Camp Joy-El. And while you could pay for a week's attendance in the Summer, most of us "earned" our way through verse memorization. This program gave us a foundation of 300 verses.

As part of my memorization recently, I came upon this verse from Leviticus 10:3. It says, *"I will display my holiness through those who come near me. I will display my glory before all the people."* I had been working at putting this truth in my mind for days when God's Spirit brought out a fascinating insight. Notice the words "through" and "to."

Let's reread it with that in mind. God will display this holiness "through" those who draw near Him.

This was true at the time of Jesus' birth, and it's true today. The hearts that were blessed at and around the manger scene—were those who came seeking the Christ-child. And the Holy Spirit of God cannot operate in and through our lives—unless—we are in constant communion with our Abba Daddy. I can think of no better way to do this than by reading His holy Word and memorizing verses from it.

Leviticus 10:3 goes on to say that the Lord will display His glory to all the people. Again, the glory of the Lord shone round about the shepherd's field. It shines forth in all of creation. God's glory is evident in a beautiful sunrise, a meadow of wildflowers, the flight of a seagull, or the glittering, starry canopy above our heads each night. In other words, as Romans 1:20 says, God has gifted us with creation so that no one would miss Him.

But it's only by drawing near the Lord, coming near, and having an intimate relationship that we learn to know God. This is how we learn to understand what pleases Him, how to obey Him, and love and serve Him and others.

God's glory is on display in His Word from Genesis to Revelation. It's on display in creation, every life form, and every living, growing thing He's made. It purely shone on one Holy Night at Bethlehem to set the stage for Jesus' mission and ministry of love at the Cross. Have you experienced His glory alone or holiness in and through you? For that's the gift of the season that brings lasting joy to every day, year, and eternally. Will you put God's Word in your mind and heart—as part of drawing near Him? Will you share His love, so others are drawn to Him and invited into His family?

Here are a few Holy Places to Pause in the Lord's Presence ...
then listen to what the Spirit speaks to your heart.

- Draw near to God: James 4:8, Psalm 65:4, Psalm 145:18.
- God's Spirit moves and works through us: Galatians 2:20, Philippians 2:13, John 15:5, Philippians 1:6.
- God's glory is displayed to everyone, and everyone will bow before Him: Isaiah 66:23-23, Philippians 2:8-9, Psalm 96:8-10.

....
....
....
....
....
....
....
....
....
....
....
....
....
....
....
....
....
....
....
....
....
....
....
....
....
....

The Lord's omnipotence made it All!

"The Lord made the earth by his power. He used his wisdom to build [establish] the world and his understanding to stretch out the skies [heavens; Prov. 3:19–20; 8:22–31]." Jeremiah 51:15 EXB

Dear Lord, when I think of the beloved carol, O Holy Night, my thoughts fill with the grandeur of Your creations. You formed the heavens, earth, the starry host and separated the light from darkness—with a spoken word.

You established it all from Your glory, power, and radiance. Your majesty is on display day and night, and I don't want to miss anything You have to share. Each one whets my appetite for what's in store in eternity with You. Amen.

<u>Pause in the Word</u>: *Please look up Psalm 19:1, Amos 5:8, Genesis 1:1, Isaiah 40:26, and Daniel 12:3. How do these "creation verses" instill a sense of awe in your heart?*

....
....
....

Beholding God's creations with a sense of awe makes us aware of His holiness, love, wisdom, and never-ending power, not just at Christmastime but every day. If you have a small view of God, your trust in Him will be limited. At the same time, an expansive view of God yields a growing, maturing faith!

Give Thanks; the Lord is Good!

"Oh, give thanks to the Lord, for He is good! For His mercy endures forever. ... To Him who made great lights, For His mercy endures forever—The sun to rule by day, for His mercy endures forever; the moon and stars to rule by night, for His mercy endures forever."
Psalm 136:1 & 7-9 NKJV

"Where is the newborn king of the Jews? We saw his star as it rose and have come to worship him."
Matthew 2:2 NLT

Father God, looking up at the night sky never ceases to amaze me. There's something about Your glittering atmosphere that draws my mind to praise. I cherish that Your thoughts toward us—outnumber the stars in the heavens, and Isaiah 40:26 tells us You call each one by name. I can only imagine the response of the Wisemen and shepherds in the field as they watched Your star—rising—to stand over Your birthplace. It drew them like magnets to know Your majesty and to worship Your great renown. And I love how the moon and stars are given to us as signs of Your mercy and unending love. How precious this is, Lord. What comfort we glean from this promise! We bring our praise as an offering, as the Wisemen brought You gold, frankincense, and myrrh. May our worship rise like incense to Your throne. Amen.

Will we be like the Wisemen who followed a star and brought gifts—seeking Jesus? How will we worship this Messiah, Who is the Savior of the world?

Known and Loved by God

"Lord, You have searched me and known me. You know when I sit down and when I get up; You understand my thoughts from far away. You scrutinize my path and my lying down, and are acquainted with all my ways. ... Darkness and light are alike to You. ... How precious also are Your thoughts for me, God! How vast is the sum of them! Were I to count them, they would outnumber the sand." Psalm 139:1-18 excerpts.

Abba Daddy, it's the middle of the night. My thoughts are jumbled, and I'm restless. I'm using this time as I usually do—to recite Your precious Word and talk to You about the needs of others. I'm lifting up friends and loved ones in these wee hours. And I've come to count this time as precious between us. What once was seen as a lack of sleep has become my dearest space of communion with You. It's where I know You're listening, and I can hear You speak. In the shadowy stillness, I can feel Your presence and know You're thinking of me—aware of my bowed posture. I'm overwhelmed by Your attention and love, and care. And I'm comforted by Your thoughts, O God, in the night— like the number of lustrous stars, like grains of sand, and in their depth and breadth. How blessed I am to be called Your child. Amen.

Take a moment to picture the night sky or your favorite beach. Close your eyes. Imagine it. Now think of this in terms of God's care toward You. It's endless—just like His love. Now let that wrap around you like an embrace. You've just had a "good night hug"—from God!

Meditate Day and Night

"This Book of the Law shall not depart from your mouth, but you shall read [and meditate on] it day and night, so that you may be careful to do [everything] in accordance with all that is written in it; for then you will make your way prosperous, and then you will be successful." Joshua 1:8 AMP

Dear Jehovah, I had been working on memorizing this verse for a few nights in a row (as is my habit twice a day) when I had this thought: Joshua 1:8 gives us a way to make every night holy. Meditating on Your Word before we go to sleep—improves our mood, sleep patterns, and well-being—simply because we're drawing near to You.

Lord, let these truths sink deeply into our consciousness. Let them become like the roots of a tree that help us thrive to develop green leaves. And help us—as we store Your Word in our hearts—to apply them daily so that they yield, obedience, we pray. Amen.

Pause in the Word: Please look up I Peter 2:2, Psalm 119:114, Proverbs 30:5, Colossians 3:16, and Psalm 119:11. Choose one and commit it to memory!

....
....

If God's Word is precious to us—and imprinted within us—it becomes a means for us to put down roots of faithfulness and, thus, develop a pattern of obedience unto the Lord.

I Lie Awake Thinking of You

"I lie awake thinking of you, meditating on you through the night. Because you are my helper, I sing for joy in the shadow of your wings." Psalm 63:6-7 NLT

Dear Jesus, I need You by day; I need You at night. I love to meditate on Who You are, what You've done for me, and how You transform my life daily. But there is something about the darkness that brings out both the struggles more vividly and my need for You more acutely. Both seem to be magnified in the shadows. My worries or concerns grow larger. But so, too, my drawing near to rely on You. This push/pull challenges me to bring You everything to Your throne. It's helped me see You as My Helper, Comforter, Defender, Rock, and Refuge.

In the wee hours, I've come to know a "wakeful rest" by coming under the shelter of Your wings. Here, I often sing Your praises in my mind, quote and pray through Scripture, and dwell with You. And before I know it ... I've drifted off to dreamland. Amen.

....
....
....

If you find yourself lying awake at night for any reason —switch Your focus from the earthly—to Your heavenly Father. Give Him praise. Lay down Your burdens. Bring Him your requests. Use hymns or Scripture to draw near to Him. Then rest in the shelter of His wings. There is no safer place to dwell!

The Desire of our Souls

"Yes, in the way of Your judgments, O Lord, we have waited for You; the desire of our soul is for Your name and for the remembrance of You. With my soul I have desired You in the night, yes, by my spirit within me I will seek You early; for when Your judgments are in the earth, the world's inhabitants will learn righteousness."
Isaiah 26:8-9 NKJV

Holy God, I desire to know You more and more each day. I hunger and thirst to be filled with Your Spirit daily and for Your strength and holiness to empower me to fulfill Your Will. My soul cries out with a longing to praise You and to draw from the fount of Your grace and blessing.

Thank You for Your protection during nighttime and for waking me to a new day with fresh opportunities to serve You. I love You, Lord, and seek to walk in Your ways. Clothe me with Your righteousness and help me put on the virtues of compassion, gentleness, humility, patience, and kindness so that I emulate Your love. Amen.

....
....
....

If we have an attitude such as this: "In the morning, in the evening, my desire is for You, God,"... the Lord will not only draw near to us, but He'll fill us with His Spirit so that we are vessels, pouring out His attributes to others.

Incline Your Ear, O Lord.

"O Lord, God of my salvation, I have cried out day and night before You. Let my prayer come before You; incline Your ear to my cry." Psalm 88:1-2 NASB

"Will not God bring about justice for His elect who cry to Him day and night, and will He delay long over them?" Luke 18:7 NASB

This song of Korah's descendants — is sometimes the cry of our heart, Lord. In times of hurt, loss, disappointment, etc., we bring everything because we trust You — the audience of One — as our Creator, Comforter, Rock, and Refuge. We draw comfort in You as our Savior and also in the blessed gift of our Salvation. We find solace in the hope that our faith brings and to which we profess. And we bring every prayer, every plea, and every praise before You, knowing that You hear us.

Incline Your ear, Jesus, because it's our heart's desire to be like Your beloved Disciples — learning, growing, and ready to share Your love and Gospel message with our little part of the world. As Your "elect" — Your sons and daughters — we're listening for Your voice and are ready and willing to obey. Amen.

Sometimes we cry out to people and later regret it. That's never the case with Jesus. Cry out to Him. He'll never betray you, gossip, or let you down. He'll love you, lift you, forgive you, and encourage you to get back up and start again. He's listening right now!

He will Shelter and Protect His Own

"For this reason, they are [standing] before the throne of God; and they serve Him [in worship] day and night in His temple; and He who sits on the throne will spread His tabernacle over them and shelter and protect them [with His presence]." Revelation 7:15 AMP

Lord God, how my heart rejoices at the image that these words portray. Those who have endured the tribulation are described in this verse as standing before You — serving and worshiping You day and night. You are described as sitting on Your throne — protecting and sheltering them by Your holy power. I love these types of passages in Revelation — where praise is the theme — and all of the saints and angels and Your children are described as exalting You.

I can only imagine the heavenly chorus, the sound as this immense number of Your children encircle You with adoration. It makes me long for that day. It gives me hope and brings me courage. I lift my praise in the day, at night, today, and always. Amen.

In the space below, form your heartfelt praise.

....
....
....

Praise brings us into God's presence, protective embrace, and company at all hours. Now, that's a promise!

A Meditation about the Hallelujah Chorus

Hallelujah—means to "Praise ye the Lord." It is an exclamation of joy, praise, gratitude, adoration, or thanksgiving to God. It's a noun used as a "shout" and a verb (or interjection) when it's a form of action.

Luke 2:21-37 concludes with the praise of a devout and righteous man named Simeon. He was present at the Temple when Mary and Joseph came to have Jesus dedicated when He was only eight days old.

Let's read verses 22-37. *"And when the days of their purification according to the law of Moses were finished, they brought Him up to Jerusalem to present Him to the Lord (just as it is written in the law of the Lord: Every firstborn male will be dedicated to the Lord and to offer a sacrifice (according to what is stated in the law of the Lord: a pair of turtledoves or two young pigeons."*

Simeon's Prophetic Praise: *"There was a man in Jerusalem whose name was Simeon. This man was righteous and devout, looking forward to Israel's consolation, and the Holy Spirit was on him. It had been revealed to him by the Holy Spirit that he would not see death before he saw the Lord's Messiah. Guided by the Spirit, he entered the temple complex. When the parents brought in the child Jesus to perform for Him what was customary under the law, Simeon took Him up in his arms, praised God, and said: Now, Master, ... my eyes have seen Your salvation. You have prepared it in the presence of all peoples—a light for revelation to the Gentiles and glory to Your people Israel. His father and mother were amazed at what was being said about Him. Then Simeon blessed them and told His mother Mary: 'Indeed, this child is destined to cause the fall and rise of many in Israel and to be a sign that will be opposed—and a sword will pierce your own soul—that the thoughts of many hearts may be revealed.'"*

Anna's Testimony *"There was also a prophetess, Anna, a daughter of Phanuel, of the tribe of Asher. She was well along in years, having lived with her husband seven years after her marriage, and was a widow for 84 years. She did not leave the temple complex, serving God night and day with fasting and prayers."* *(HCSB)*

The Holy Spirit had revealed to Simeon that he would not die until he had seen Jesus. This was fulfilled as he held the Christ-child in his arms and blessed God. Anna, who was also present at this traditional celebration, added her adoration. She was a widow who served in the Temple, praying and serving the Lord.

From verse 38—*"At that very moment, she came up and began to thank God and to speak about Him to all who were looking forward to the redemption of Jerusalem."* *(HCSB)*

When everything was performed according to the Law, Mary, Joseph, and Jesus returned to Galilee to the village of Nazareth. Jesus grew, increasing in spiritual wisdom, and the grace of God was upon Him.

As we conclude *There's a Song in the Air*, I can't help but think that praise must have echoed in the atmosphere that filled the Temple at Jesus' dedication. It must have also been the emotion of Mary's heart as she and her little family returned home. And as we celebrate this beloved season of Jesus' birth, I hope you, too, experience a sense of His worth and majesty. I hope you spend some time pondering and beholding Who He is. The Lord God is omnipotent. He is Almighty. He reigns on high in the corridors of heaven and in the heart of every Christ-follower who calls Him Lord. He is eternal. And He deserves every hallelujah that we can raise.

Will we be like Simeon, who could not wait to know Jesus, to meet Him, and to express our adoration like an offering? Will we be like Anna, who served in the Temple and came to bow and love her King? And will we—with every carol that we hear or sing in this holy season—exalt Jesus so highly that we are found seeking Him in His Temple always, as these verses from Psalms proclaim?

"Hallelujah! My soul, praise the Lord. I will praise the Lord all my life; I will sing to my God as long as I live." Psalm 146:1-2 HCSB

Of note? Psalm 106:1, 111:1, 112:1, 113:1, 117:1, 135:1, and 147:1 all begin with the words; *"Praise ye the Lord."* Notice that each praise begins with verse 1, which encourages us to look to the One Who rules with all authority, dominion, power, justice, hope, peace, and love. And I highly encourage you to look each of these verses up, and here's a little space to ponder ....

Revelation 19:1 points to a future time when every child of God will raise hallelujahs to His name: *"After this I heard something like the loud voice of a vast multitude in heaven, saying: Hallelujah! Salvation, glory, and power belong to our God (HCSB)."*

Merry Christmas and Happy New Year!
deb and doug

With Dedication

Dear Jesus,
This is our offering of love, gratitude, and praise. May every prayer and Pray-it-Through Scriptural meditation bring us near to Your throne.

Dear Douglas,
I offer you a heartfelt "thank you." This has been a fun project to work on together. You're my best friend, and my earthly and heavenly treasure! I love you and cherish every day of our journey. Thank you for every special Christmas (no matter where we spent it)!

Dear Family and Friends, we appreciate your support and notes of encouragement, and hope you enjoy our latest endeavor.

In loving memory of my Mom, *Pauline Rubeck Goshorn,* thank you for your example of faith and love for the Lord. We celebrate your cherishing of Christmas and Jesus' birth. Thank you for making the reading of Luke 2, a beloved tradition in our home, that we still emulate.

I am grateful to each of you, and my readers, and I pray that *There's a Song in the Air* Devotional will bring you blessings and joy!

In His Love, *deborah goshorn-stenger*

We hope this holy holiday season is filled with joy, carols, and a spirit of Christ's love. It's our prayer that you'll experience the nearness of Immanuel—God with us—within your heart and home and with your family, friends, neighbors, co-workers, and even strangers. Because the hope, peace, and grace of His coming—only becomes a gift to us if He is present in our own lives—and then we share Him as our gift to the world. Blessings!

"And this is the testimony: God has given us eternal life, and this life is in his Son." 1 John 5:11 NIV

Dear Readers,

Now that you've finished our *There's a Song in the Air Devotional* it would mean the world to us if you left us a thoughtful **Review** on Amazon. Did you enjoy the meditations – did they speak to your heart? Did the Christmas-themed sketch art add to the enjoyment of the book? What would you like to see more of? To let a **Review,** simply point your phone camera at the QR code (to the left), which will take you directly to our Amazon review page.

We would love for you to **Check out our Website** (using the QR code to the right), where you can enjoy Weekly Inspirations, see more of our story, and sign up for our Mailing List.

As always: "The Lord bless you and keep you; the Lord make His face shine upon you, and be gracious to you; the Lord lift up His countenance upon you, and give you peace." Numbers 6:24-26 NKJV

deb and doug

Also By Deborah Goshorn-Stenger

The Creation's Kaleidoscope Series

The Devotional Word Search Puzzle Book Series

The Purry Companion's Series

You can find all the details on books in these series, and more at:

www.2PauseandPraiseCreations.com/Books

or simply point your phone camera at the QR code (below), which will take you directly to our Website Books page.

Your Free Book is Waiting!

Are you seeking to develop a more intimate Prayer Life with Jesus? Do you want to know what God's Word says about Prayer? Then this beautifully illustrated book is for you!

This "Pray-it-Through" verse style of Devotional combines a Word Search Puzzle, Sketch Art, and full-size Coloring Pages to create an innovative way 2 Pause and Praise the Lord. This 72-page offering is a prequel for Deb's other full-size Word Search Puzzle Books. On Wings of Prayer will deepen your conversations with the Lord. Here, you'll be encouraged to get into God's Word and sink His precious truths into your heart!

Get your free copy of
On Wings of Prayer here:

We hope you've enjoyed the exploration of Jesus' birth through these Carol Titles and God's precious Word. Please use the QR code (right) to visit our Website.

46573017R00070